I SENT YOU TO REAP

RILEY STEPHENSON

**KENNETH
COPELAND
PUBLICATIONS**

I Sent You to Reap

ISBN 978-1-60463-218-7

30-0823

17 16 15 14 13 12

7 6 5 4 3 2

© 2012 Riley Stephenson

Kenneth Copeland Publications
Fort Worth, TX 76192-0001

For more information about Kenneth Copeland Ministries, visit kcm.org or call 1-800-600-7395 (U.S. only) or +1-817-852-6000.

Table of Contents

Introduction v

1. Reasons Christians Don't Witness 1

2. How to Win Souls 19

3. The Power of God's Word to Save 41

4. Discipleship After the Decision— 57
   How to Follow Up With New Believers

5. Setting 'Soul Goals' 67

6. Witnessing to Your Family 75

Conclusion 81

Introduction

Some Christians long to experience what it must have been like living in "Bible days." They fail to realize that we who are alive today are destined to see even greater things than those who have gone before us. These *are* Bible days—in fact, we're living in the greatest times on planet Earth!

However, we're not going to see those greater things without obeying God's Word and stepping out to do the same works those early believers did in the Name of Jesus. The early saints were ablaze with passion for the heart of God. And, His heart has always been about the harvest—the precious fruit of people's souls gathered into His kingdom (James 5:7). I have devoted my life and ministry to this very work.

"But, why place so much emphasis on soul-winning, Riley? Aren't we simply supposed to be light to a darkened world? Isn't that enough?"

Certainly, there should be such a difference between the believer and unbeliever, that unbelievers are prompted to seek the light of God in us, whether or not they even recognize it's God they're seeking. However, in seeking the light, they're actually seeking out believers. We are the carriers of the light of Life, Jesus Christ! Not only should we be ready when they come, but we should be proactive in obedience to the Scriptures by seeking out the unbeliever. In other words, the harvest isn't going to come to us, we must go to the harvest. We've been sent out—*commissioned*—to reap it (Mark 16:15)!

In recent years, I've noticed a seeming decline in our efforts to reach out beyond "our four walls" of our churches to a lost and dying world around us. I'm not talking about statistics concerning those sent ones—missionaries who are laying down their lives ministering in other nations of the world. I'm talking about individual believers testifying of our Lord in "Jerusalem, and in all Judea and Samaria"—in other words, their local neighborhoods, communities, cities and nations, as well as to the ends of the earth. (See Acts 1:8.)

The Body of Christ, especially in the western world, has apparently fallen asleep or become complacent and desensitized regarding lost and dying souls who are slipping out into a dark eternity without God. Certainly, there are "pockets" of evangelism taking place, but as a whole, it seems our passion and fire for the lost has diminished to just a tiny flame.

We should be burning so brightly and be so on fire for God that we impact lives for eternity every day, everywhere we go! Jesus said to the church at Laodicea—and it can certainly apply to the Church today—"So then because thou art lukewarm, and neither cold nor hot, I will spue [spew] thee out of my mouth" (Revelation 3:16, *KJV*). In the preceding verse, He said, "I know thy works, that thou art neither cold nor hot: I would thou wert cold or hot" (verse 15). I don't know about you, but I'm always checking my spiritual temperature! I don't want to make Jesus vomit because of my complacency and self-satisfaction, while His desires, will and plan become unimportant and insignificant in my life.

So why emphasize souls? Souls are the heart and plan of God. It's a great miracle of God when someone is born again—his spirit gloriously re-created and made brand new by God's Spirit. And, to be the messenger for someone's salvation is an amazing experience beyond words to describe. It's "...joy unspeakable and full of glory" (1 Peter 1:8, *KJV*)!

The purpose of this book is not to condemn, if you've lost your passion for God and His desire for a harvest of souls—but to guide you in regaining the fire and spiritual momentum you're going to need for the days ahead. There is a great ingathering of souls that must take place before Christ's return, and He has sent you to take your own unique place in reaping those souls!

Yours in the harvest,

Riley

CHAPTER 1

REASONS CHRISTIANS DON'T WITNESS

And then he [Jesus] told them, "Go into all the world and preach the Good News to everyone, everywhere."

Mark 16:15, *NLT*

In talking with believers through the years, I have come to the conclusion that most don't witness or share the gospel with the unsaved on a regular basis. In questioning them further, I have also discovered *why* they don't actively participate in what is commonly referred to as the "Great Commission" in Mark 16:15. What holds them back from acting on, or obeying, the truth they know?

In this chapter, we're going to look at five main reasons Christians don't witness about Jesus to the unsaved: (1) fear; (2) believing too much in their own excuses; (3) the mistaken belief that they must be specially "led" to witness; (4) the incorrect notion that they must be specifically called to "sow" or "reap," but not both; and (5) feelings that they must be more spiritually prepared before they can effectively witness.

Reason No. 1: The Fear Factor

Let's look in greater detail at Jesus' "Great Commission" to His Church:

> And He said to them, "Go into all the world and preach the gospel to every creature. He who believes and is baptized will be saved; but he who does not believe will be condemned. And these signs will follow those who believe: In My name they will cast out demons; they will speak with new tongues; they will take up serpents; and if they drink anything deadly, it will by no means hurt them; they will lay hands on the sick, and they will recover" (Mark 16:15-18).

Although the Bible is clear concerning the Great Commission, as we've seen, most Christians are not doing it. They're goodhearted believers who love God, but they're not fulfilling His command to share the good news about Jesus with the lost.

First John 5:3 says, "For this is the love of God, that we keep His commandments. And His commandments are not burdensome." Obeying God's Word is not burdensome or hard. In fact, it's easy. The Bible says that the way of the *sinner* is hard, but the believer wears an easy yoke. (See Proverbs 13:15; Matthew 11:30.)

Simply put, God would never tell us to do something we were incapable of doing. So, the next time someone suggests you share the good news to someone about Jesus, instead of saying, "I can't," say, *"I can!"* After all Philippians 4:13 says: "I can do *all* things through Christ who strengthens me." You *can* tell others the good news of the gospel. That good news is "the power of God to salvation" to those who will believe it (Romans 1:16). It is the very power of God Himself to translate them from the kingdom of darkness into the Kingdom of light!

Then, why are so many disobeying God's easy command to witness to others about His saving grace? Fear. In fact, fear is the major reason Christian don't witness.

If believers were to openly confess the fears they've been nurturing (even unintentionally) about witnessing, we'd hear things like:

> "I'm afraid of what the person will think of me."

> "I'm afraid of what my friends might say."

> "I'm afraid I'll be rejected."

> "I'm afraid of what my parents (or family members) will say."

> "I'm afraid my co-workers will talk about me behind my back."

Fear has been a huge problem among believers that has affected their willingness to step out of their "comfort zone" to obey God. And, I think we can all say we've experienced this fear in some form and to some degree. But, thankfully, as believers, we have the Bible—the Word of God—which addresses this issue of fear.

For example:

> Romans 8:31 says, "'If God is for us, who can be against us?'"

> Romans 8:37 says, "We are more than conquerors through Him who loved us."

> First Corinthians 2:16 says, "We have the mind of Christ."

God's Word is Him speaking to us, and every word of God is true! Most Christians would agree with that, and most Christians know the scriptures I just listed. They know they don't need to be afraid. They know they *shouldn't* be afraid. Then what's the problem? They don't understand the true source of fear or how to stand against it when it comes (and it will try to come to all of us at some time or another).

Where's That Fear Coming From?

"God has not given us a spirit of fear and timidity, but of power, love, and self-discipline. So never be ashamed to tell others about our Lord. And don't be ashamed of me, either, even though I'm in prison for him. With the strength God gives you, be ready to suffer with me for the sake of the Good News" (2 Timothy 1:7-8, *NLT*).

These verses let us know that fear doesn't come from God. Fear is an evil spirit. It comes from the enemy, Satan—the devil—and it comes because he doesn't want us to share our faith or to step out in faith in *any* area to obey the Lord.

Since we know that fear doesn't come from God, what *does* come from Him, according to this passage in 2 Timothy is *power, love* and *self-discipline*. In other words, you *do* have the power to witness! You have the love to witness! And, you have the self-discipline to witness! All that's left is *to choose to witness!*

What Fear Can Do

Proverbs 29:25 *(KJV)* says, "The fear of man bringeth a snare: but whoso putteth his trust in the Lord shall be safe." Fear can *trap* us. It can hold us captive and completely "paralyze" or render us inoperative and ineffective.

The *New Living Translation* says, "Fearing people is a dangerous trap, but trusting the Lord means safety." So, if we're afraid of what someone else thinks about us, that fear can snare us and keep us back from doing what we're supposed to do. Giving place to fear of what others might say or how they might respond will probably keep you from witnessing to them about the Lord.

Let me break this down for you, so you'll understand that you're not alone. Let's suppose you're out doing street evangelism. You see this big guy who looks as if he could be a bodybuilder. You feel a tug in your heart to witness to him, but, suddenly, thoughts begin to flood your mind: *Man, that guy could chew me up and spit me out if he wanted to! Maybe I should just leave him alone.*

Where do you think those thoughts are coming from? I'll give you a hint: The Lord would never say, "He's so big! You'd better not tell him about My Son. Don't tell him about Jesus' shed blood. Don't share with that man how much I love him. That unction would not be of Me!"

Anytime you hear a "voice" telling you not to witness, or you have thoughts that make you afraid to witness, with great boldness and confidence, you can cast them down, in Jesus' Name. You can say, "No, Devil, I stand against your spirit of fear. I *will* witness to others about Jesus!"

What Love Can Do

We have seen what fear can do—what power it can have in the life of a believer if he or she yields to it. But since we know fear doesn't come from God, we know we can *resist* fear and refuse to yield to it.

Let's look again at 2 Timothy 1:7 *(NLT):* "God has not given us a spirit of fear and timidity, but of power, love, and self-discipline." God has given us *power, love* and *self-discipline* for living—not a spirit of fear that makes us want to cringe or hide! Let's focus on that middle word, *love,* for a moment. What is love? First and foremost, the Bible says that *God* is love (1 John 4:8).

Let's look at just a few verses that show what love can do:

Love covers all sins (Proverbs 10:12).

And above all things have fervent love for one another,

for "love will cover a multitude of sins" (1 Peter 4:8).

There is no fear in love; but perfect love casts out fear,
because fear involves torment. But he who fears has
not been made perfect in love (1 John 4:18).

You see, if we're yielding to the love of God that's in our hearts as believers (Romans 5:5), we will want to see people's sins remitted. We will
want to see them born again, restored to a right relationship with God,
and destined for heaven when they die and their spirit leaves this earth.

Go therefore and make disciples of all the nations,
baptizing them in the name of the Father and of the
Son and of the Holy Spirit, teaching them to observe
all things that I have commanded you; and lo, I am
with you always, even to the end of the age. Amen
(Matthew 28:19-20).

As believers, we have the Holy Spirit, the divine ability to witness and share Jesus with others, the love of God in our hearts,
power and self-discipline. In fact, God has given us everything we
need to obey His commission to witness, win the lost and to make
disciples (teach new believers). Jesus, the Son of Love, is with us.
We have nothing to fear!

Provision and Protection

Someone said, "I understand that. But what if my fear has nothing
to do with what people think of me? I'm just afraid of getting hurt! *I
don't want to be beaten up!*"

Certainly, there are those, especially in other nations in the world,
who will be martyred for their faith. But Paul wrote those inspired
words to Timothy, pastor of the church in Ephesus, at a time when
religious persecution by tyrannical government rulers was at an all-time

high. Yet he exhorted them not to fear! We as believers have God's provision when we step out to obey Him, and we also have His *protection*.

Consider this:

> The Lord is on my side; I will not fear. What can man do to me? (Psalm 118:6).
>
> God's now at my side…who would dare lay a hand on me? (Psalm 118:6, *MSG*).
>
> The righteous person faces many troubles, but the Lord comes to the rescue each time. For the Lord protects them from harm—not one of their bones will be broken! (Psalm 34:19-20, *NLT*).
>
> He guards the paths of justice, and preserves the way of His saints (Proverbs 2:8).
>
> So we may boldly say: "The Lord is my helper; I will not fear. What can man do to me?" (Hebrews 13:6).

I also encourage you to read Psalm 91. It was written by the psalmist David about divine protection. I encourage you to read it from several different translations and to meditate on it continually so it sinks deep into your heart and stays there.

Divine protection belongs to us as believers. In fact, in many places in the New Testament, one of the words for *salvation* is "protection." You may have heard some horror stories about people witnessing and some strange things happening. But, I've been leading soul-winning teams—as well as witnessing on my own—for many years, and I promise you, not one of my bones has ever been broken!

The closest I've ever come to being assaulted was years ago in downtown Fort Worth, Texas. I was walking alongside a fence outside a patio restaurant and bar. Sometimes there's a lot of partying going on outside on that patio! I handed a man a tract, and he grabbed me from the other side of the fence, which was about waist high, and put me in a headlock! He wasn't trying to hurt me, he was just trying to be funny in front of his friends. I hand out tracts at that particular restaurant quite often, so one of his friends recognized me and said, "Hey, this guy's a minister."

The man who had me "captive" immediately let me go and said, "Oh, I'm so sorry!" I talked to both friends, and they ended up getting saved that day! And none of my bones was broken! In fact, I wasn't even bruised!

You can pray for God's protection before you go out to witness, and you can claim God's promises in Psalm 91 that you won't be touched or harmed. Actually, the worst, *and saddest*, thing that can happen when you're out witnessing is not the threat of harm, but having someone tell you he doesn't want the Savior.

OK, Now What? How Do I Get Free From Fear?

As a child of God, you have authority over the spirit of fear. You can stand against it until it holds no more sway or authority over your life, which belongs completely to God.

Psalm 34:4 *(NLT)* says:

> I prayed to the Lord, and he answered me, He freed me from all my fears.

So, what should you do to overcome fear? The first thing you need to do is pray to the Lord, and He'll answer. He'll free you from every fear.

In the Bible, we often see that anyone who received from God had to cooperate with Him by demonstrating faith. One of the ways we cooperate with God today and show ourselves to be in agreement with Him and His Word is to talk about or "confess" His Word.

If you've experienced fear about witnessing to others about Jesus that you've struggled to overcome, pray this prayer and then repeat the following *confession* out loud every chance you get—morning, noon and night. Remember, God's Word is His power unto salvation (protection, deliverance or *whatever* you need) to those who believe (Romans 1:16). And, faith to receive and walk in the fullness of God's best comes by hearing the Word of God (Romans 10:17).

Prayer:

Lord, according Your Word in Psalm 34:4, I am praying to You. Free me from the fear of witnessing to others about Your Son. Your Word says You'll answer me and free from this fear. Thank You for hearing and answering me, in Jesus' Name. Thank You that I'm free!

Confession:

God has not given me a spirit of fear. He's given me power, love and self-discipline. I can do all things through Christ who strengthens me. I am strong in the Lord and the power of His might. I may feel weak, but I SAY that I'm strong. I have been delivered from the power of darkness through Jesus, the Son of God's love, and I am the righteousness of God. The wicked flee when no one's pursuing them, but the righteous are as bold as a lion. I do not "flee" or hide from witnessing. I am as bold as a lion. In Jesus' Name!

(SCRIPTURES: 2 Timothy 1:7; Philippians 4:13; Ephesians 6:10; Joel 3:10; Colossians 1:13; 2 Corinthians 5:21; Proverbs 28:1)

Stand Down Fear by Stepping Out in Faith

One time, I took a group out witnessing, and we began telling people about Jesus in the parking lot at a particular location. We first shared with a young man, who rededicated his life to the Lord and was healed right there in the parking lot!

We walked a little more, when I noticed that a girl in our group was lagging behind. Everyone else was excited, but she was really quiet as if deep in thought. Soon, she made her way to the front of the crowd and said to me, "Riley, I don't know about all this. I think I'm just going to stay at the back of the group and pray for everyone else."

"That's fine, Michelle. You can do that," I said.

We began talking to another young man, and after sharing a couple of scriptures with him, I said to him, "By the way, Michelle would like to lead you in a quick prayer."

Right then and there, this very shy, timid girl led that young man in a prayer for salvation. Afterward, she could hardly contain her excitement! Fear could no longer hold her in bondage once she confronted that fear and dealt with it by stepping out in faith.

Reason No. 2: 'It's Raining, I'm Broke, My Cat's Sick....'

As we saw, the first big reason many believers don't witness is *fear*. The second reason is *excuses*. In other words, it's too easy for Christians to make excuses and to believe those excuses are legitimate reasons why they can't obey the Great Commission. These Christians are as sincere as they can be when they back out of their commitment to go out witnessing. They'll say, for example, "Well, it looks like rain tonight." Or, "I need every bit of gas in my car to get to work and back." Or, "My cat [or pet] is sick. I need to stay home and watch it sleep"!

First, let me say that, of course, there are times when legitimate things occur in our lives that prevent us from doing what we've planned. This is not to criticize or put anyone under condemnation. I'm simply exposing this mechanism of "excuse-making" because it can be a subtle trick of the enemy to lure and lull us into a complacent state of mind until the excuses become easier and easier. Pretty soon, our passion for the lost is gone. Let's all be keenly aware of the way the enemy operates so we don't fall prey to his devices or schemes (2 Corinthians 2:11).

One thing I've made up my mind about is to witness to people about Jesus despite weather conditions. Unless the National Weather Service has issued an emergency alert, I take teams out to witness when we're scheduled to go. If it's raining or snowing outside, we witness inside! We won't allow the weather to deter us because the unsaved can accept Christ outside or inside!

One evening, we scheduled a team to go witnessing, but the weather was very stormy on that particular night. One person who had signed up to go with us called to say he couldn't attend because of the weather. I'd heard the weather report, and I purposely hadn't canceled the outreach because I was determined to fulfill the commission on my life as a believer to proclaim the gospel to the unsaved. I knew we'd spend most of the evening indoors at various places in the city; therefore, the outreach was scheduled to continue as planned.

After I hung up the phone, the Lord spoke to my spirit. He said, *Riley, it's storming in people's lives tonight, and you have the answer.* That night, approximately 75 people prayed to receive Jesus and were born again!

What if we had all stayed home?

Questions We Must Each Answer for Ourselves

As an evangelism team leader, I don't allow my feelings to get hurt when I have a low turnout on a particular outreach. But, in my teachings, I like to encourage people to stop making excuses to not go out with the team.

As I mentioned, I've heard people say, "Well, I don't have extra gas money. I need that gas to get to work." Yet some of those same people will fast, pray, believe God and use their faith against all odds when they want or need extra money for something else!

In other words, these people will gladly acknowledge that they're kings and priests unto God, more than conquerors, overcomers, delivered, redeemed and blessed above all people of the earth. But, they only put those truths into practice in some areas of their lives—not in all areas.

So, when it comes to sacrificing our time and other resources to share our faith with the lost, we need to ask ourselves: "Am I making this as important in my life as other things I allocate time and money toward?" The answer to that question will help us have the right perspective the next time we're tempted to use an excuse we know deep down inside us is not really legitimate.

As I said, God's commands are not grievous or burdensome—instead, they inspire joy, strength and happiness in the believer's heart. Yet the things that stand in the way to oppose our obedience are very real and must be dealt with.

I encourage you to pray the following prayer from your heart. Also, use it as a daily prayer, or alter it to make it a positive confession or affirmation of faith:

> **Lord, help me to love the things You love and to hate the things You hate. You love the salvation of people's souls—men's, women's and children's—and You hate seeing the lost perish in their sin and condemn themselves to a sinner's hell. You came to call sinners to repentance and to reconcile the world to Yourself, through the precious blood of Jesus and Your saints calling the world to repentance through His Name. It's not in my own strength, Lord, but it's You who is working in me by Your Spirit to will and to do of Your good will and pleasure. I stir myself up to pray and fellowship with You, and to seek Your glorious face so that my own heart will beat in rhythm with Yours for the lost in this world. In Jesus' Name I pray. Amen.**
>
> **(Scriptures: Matthew 9:13; Mark 2:17; Luke 5:32;**

1 Peter 1:18-19; 2 Corinthians 5:19-20; Philippians
2:13; Hebrews 10:24)

Reason No. 3: The Mistaken Belief That You Must Be Specially 'Led' to Witness

A third reason believers don't witness about Jesus as they should is the mistaken belief that *they must be specially led by God to witness.*

Some people argue that we're to win souls only as we're led by the Holy Spirit. It's true, we need to follow the leading of the Spirit in our witnessing as well as in every area of our lives. But, Acts 1:8 says, "You shall receive power when the Holy Spirit has come upon you; and *you shall be witnesses to Me* in Jerusalem, and in all Judea and Samaria, and to the end of the earth."

According to this scripture, we don't need to be specially led to witness or to win souls. When the Holy Spirit came upon us, we immediately became witnesses for Jesus! We *are* His witnesses "to the end of the earth"!

Jesus Himself said in Mark 16:15, "Go into all the world and preach the gospel to every creature." The *New Living Translation*-96 says, "Go into all the world and preach the Good News to everyone, everywhere." We don't need to hear a special word from God when He has already said in His Word to *go!*

We don't need to be specially led where God has already given us His will and command. God wants us to talk to everyone about Jesus. People's eternal destinies depend on what they do with Jesus. But how will they hear about Him unless someone preaches or proclaims Him (Romans 10:14)?

Instead of taking the attitude, "Maybe God doesn't want me to talk to that person," we should all have the mindset, *If I don't talk to that person, who will? Maybe no one.*

Reason No. 4: The Notion That
Some Are Called to Sow or Reap, But Not Both

The fourth reason believers don't witness is closely related to reason No. 3: They mistakenly believe that *some are specifically called to sow, and others to reap—but they're not usually called to do both!*

Some believers are content with the fact that they're "putting the Word out there" when they share their faith. They, in effect, believe that they are predominantly called to do the sowing—and someone else is called to do the reaping. They quote the scripture, "For in this the saying is true: 'One sows and another reaps'" (John 4:37). Others don't witness or share their faith very much at all based on this same verse, saying they don't feel called to sow *or* reap.

But let's read John 4:37 in context:

> Jesus said to them, "My food is to do the will of Him who sent Me, and to finish His work. Do you not say, 'There are still four months and then comes the harvest'? Behold, I say to you, lift up your eyes and look at the fields, for they are already white for harvest! And he who reaps receives wages, and gathers fruit for eternal life, that both he who sows and he who reaps may rejoice together. For in this the saying is true: 'One sows and another reaps'" (verses 34-37).

In 1 Corinthians 3:6, the Apostle Paul also says, "I planted, Apollos watered, but God gave the increase." Many have used these verses to contend that only certain God-ordained believers are supposed to reap the harvest of a person's soul. For example, they'll share their testimony with someone who's unsaved and say, "Well, goodbye. God bless you. Jesus loves you!" They seem content to have sown some seed into that person's life without even *attempting* to reap a harvest.

However, if you read John 4:37 in context, you'll see that Jesus is talking about a harvest field of the world *that's already ripe and ready!*

> Do you not say, "There are still four months and then comes the harvest"? Behold, I say to you, lift up your eyes and look at the fields, FOR THEY ARE ALREADY WHITE FOR HARVEST! (John 4:35).

Call Yourself a Reaper

Jesus said, "...the saying is true: 'One sows and another reaps'" (John 4:37). Then, in verse 38, He said, "I sent you to reap that for which you have not labored; others have labored, and you have entered into their labors."

Let's look at verse 38 in the *NLT:*

> I sent you to harvest where you didn't plant; others had already done the work, and now you will get to gather the harvest.

It's clear that the harvest of people's souls is ripe or ready to be harvested—and that we as Jesus' followers have been commissioned, or *sent*, to reap! So instead of allowing ourselves to think, *Maybe I'm just a sower*, we need to call ourselves *reapers* or *harvesters. God has sent us to reap!*

Reason No. 5: Feelings of Inadequacy or Feelings That You're Not Ready Spiritually

A fifth big reason believers don't share their faith in Christ is *feelings that they must be more spiritually prepared* before they can effectively witness.

Many Christians have this belief who've been saved and in church for years. They've been taught the Scriptures week in and week out.

They have forgotten more Scripture than most people know to begin with! But, they're being robbed by feelings of inadequacy that they're just not taught and trained enough to share a few scriptures.

Many Christians who have been pumped full of the Word for years still have no confidence they are who God says they are: "witnesses unto me" (Acts 1:8, *KJV)!* They've been to conventions and taken notes at every meeting. They're in church every Sunday—and probably more often than that. Yet, they're afraid they'll meet up with someone out on the street and won't know what to say.

If you feel you need special training to witness to certain religious groups, there are plenty of materials online and in print you can read. So "being trained" should not be a concern. (In fact, you're reading this book on evangelism training, so consider yourself being trained!) Remember, for all our fears, excuses, misgivings, and notions of being inadequate and inferior, one truth remains: As believers, we're called to witness about Jesus. We have been enabled by the Holy Spirit, *and* equipped with God's Word, which is His very power manifested toward those who believe (Romans 1:16; Ephesians 1:19, 3:20).

Are you saved? Do you believe? If so, you're ready to *go!* into all the world—your neighborhood, your town or community, other states or countries—and share with others the gospel, the good news, of Christ!

Don't Wait for the Preacher

And He [Jesus] Himself gave some to be apostles, some prophets, some evangelists, and some pastors and teachers, for the equipping of the saints for the work of ministry, for the edifying of the body of Christ (Ephesians 4:11-12).

When He rose from the dead, Jesus Himself gave ministry gifts, or ministry offices, to the Church—His Body. For what purpose? Verse 12 tells us: "For the equipping of the saints for the work of ministry...." That means, for one, that it's not the pastor's job to fulfill the Great Commission. The job of the pastor, teacher, apostle, evangelist and prophet is to equip the saints to fulfill their own ministry, or commission, to win souls and to train new believers.

It's a mistaken belief that you need a pulpit to witness or testify about the Lord. In fact, even full-time ministers should be soul winners outside the pulpit. They're believers, too, and the Great Commission applies to them, as well. (On the other hand, we should not leave the winning of souls to the preacher on Sunday morning.)

One time, while ministering at a Bible school, I suddenly said out of my spirit, "Pastors and ministers are depending on their pulpits to be a place to win the lost." I didn't think much further about it and ended the session. During the break, a man came up to me, crying. He said, "Brother Riley, I'm a pastor. What you said is so right. You've 'hit the nail on the head.' I've just been waiting for people to come up front to the altar to be saved. I haven't been witnessing anywhere else except behind my pulpit."

Well, *I* didn't hit the nail on the head—the Holy Ghost did! I ministered to that young pastor, and we prayed together. Later, during my time there, he testified that he led three people to the Lord in a grocery store!

My point is, you don't need Bible school or seminary training to win the lost. You don't need to read 100 books on soul winning to be qualified to share the simple gospel message. You simply need to be willing to obey God, step out in faith, and open your mouth to proclaim the truth of God's Word you already know. God will do the rest!

The first part of Ephesians 4:12 tells us why Jesus gave us pastors, teachers, missionaries, evangelists and prophets: "For the equipping of the saints for the work of ministry...." The rest of that verse tells us *why* we need to be equipped to do the work: "...for the edifying [or building up] of the body of Christ." We need to build and expand the Body of

Christ, one soul at a time, if necessary.

Protect Your Most Valuable Asset and Witnessing Tool — Your Relationship With the Lord

"The members of the council were amazed when they saw the boldness of Peter and John, for they could see that they were ordinary men who had had no special training. They also recognized them as men who had been with Jesus" (Acts 4:13, *NLT-96*).

When people looked at these two disciples and noticed the authority and confidence with which they spoke, they couldn't help but notice, too, that they were just ordinary men. But they recognized and acknowledged that these men had been with Jesus.

The same can be said about us today! When we're out among those in the world—among the unsaved—people should notice that there's something different about us because we've been with the Anointed One, Jesus Christ, and His Anointing is within and upon us.

We walk in that anointing to a stronger and stronger degree the more we spend time with Jesus, reading, studying and meditating on His Word. Any believer can do this. The anointing is not just for the preacher or teacher.

There is a sixth reason believers don't witness about the Lord as they should, and that is, *they simply don't know how!* The "how to" of soul winning is the subject of the next chapter.

CHAPTER 2

HOW TO WIN SOULS

In the last chapter, I talked primarily about five reasons Christians don't witness to the lost about Jesus. As I mentioned, there is a sixth reason that I'll cover in this chapter: *They don't know how to witness.*

Many books have been written and courses assembled on techniques for soul winning, and some of it is great material. However, some is so complicated it scares people away from sharing the gospel. But testifying about the Lord—being a witness for Him—is *easy.*

Some Christians have said to me, "Well, Riley, it's easy for you; you have the gift of evangelism. You have a special anointing to win souls."

I always answer, "I *do* have a special anointing; I'm a *believer!* You have that same anointing!" In Mark 16, it says that certain signs follow those who believe *(believers,* or *believing ones,* verse 17). If you're a *believing one,* signs will follow you when you're proclaiming God's Word and testifying about the Lord.

My Simple Method: Speak the Word and Pray

As I said, there are various methods or techniques for winning souls. I'll share with you what has worked for me for years. I witness the same way every day, using a pocket-sized card that contains the following script:[1]

> Hi, my name is _____ [GIVE YOUR FIRST NAME]. I want to ask you a few questions. Do you live in the area? Do you go to church in _____ [NAME THE PERSON'S TOWN]? _____ [REPEAT THE PERSON'S NAME], I have another question: If you died right now, where would you go?
>
> [IF HE OR SHE RESPONDS, "TO HELL," "I DON'T KNOW," OR GIVES ANY OTHER ANSWER BESIDES "HEAVEN," GO STRAIGHT TO THE SCRIPTURES THAT FOLLOW— ROMANS 3:23, ROMANS 6:23 AND ROMANS 10:13.]
>
> [IF HE OR SHE RESPONDS, "TO HEAVEN," say:] That's great, _____. Let me ask you—if God were to say to you, "Why should I let you in?" what would you tell Him?
>
> [IF THE PERSON GIVES ANY OTHER ANSWER THAN THE FOLLOWING, RESPOND:] There's only one reason why God would allow anyone to stand in His presence, and it's because Jesus took our place and died on the cross for us so that we could be saved.
>
> [NOTE: IT'S IMPORTANT NOT TO ARGUE WITH THE PERSON. IF HE/SHE SAYS, "I'M A GOOD PERSON,"

---

1 You may download the soul-winning reference card *(Pocket Reference for Soul Winning)* at: www.rileystephenson.com. Click on "Resources" to download the Adobe Acrobat (PDF) document.

"I GIVE TO THE POOR," "I GO TO CHURCH," ETC.,
YOU SHOULD SIMPLY SAY SOMETHING LIKE,
"THAT'S GREAT. WE NEED MORE GOOD PEOPLE IN
THIS WORLD." THEN, REDIRECT HIM/HER TO THE
SCRIPTURE. NEVER *ASK* IF YOU MAY READ THE
SCRIPTURE TO THE PERSON. SIMPLY *REDIRECT* THEM
TO THE WORD.]

[CONTINUE:] The Bible says, "All have sinned and fall
short of the glory of God" (Romans 3:23), and, "The
wages of sin is death, but the gift of God is eternal life
in Christ Jesus our Lord" (Romans 6:23). But, Romans
10:13 says, "Whoever calls on the name of the Lord
shall be saved."

[CONTINUE:] _____, pray this prayer
after me. "Heavenly Father, I believe Jesus died on the
cross for me and rose again [RESPONSE]. I give You
my life [RESPONSE]. I want Jesus Christ to come into
my life and into my heart. Amen [RESPONSE]."

[NOTE: IT'S EXTREMELY IMPORTANT NOT TO ASK
THE PERSON IF HE/SHE WOULD LIKE PRAYER. SOME
REAPERS AREN'T COMFORTABLE JUST SAYING,
"PRAY THIS PRAYER WITH ME," SO, INSTEAD, THEY'LL
ASK, "WOULD YOU LIKE TO PRAY WITH ME?" IT'S
IMPORTANT TO *GUIDE* THE UNSAVED PERSON IN
PRAYER INSTEAD OF ASKING IF HE'D LIKE TO PRAY.]

'I Don't Want to Be Pushy— What If They're Not Ready?'

When you're sharing the gospel with someone who's unsaved, that
person is not familiar with the things of God. It's human nature that
the person will likely "bail," or avoid praying with you, if given the

chance. That's why I never ask, "Would you like to pray with me?" Or, "May I pray with you?"

First Corinthians 2:14 says:

> But the natural man does not receive the things of the Spirit of God, for they are foolishness [meaningless nonsense] to him; nor can he know them, because they are spiritually discerned.

When I first started witnessing, I would ask people, "May I pray with you?" I heard every answer from, "No, I'm just here at the store to buy some tomatoes," to "I'm just here at Starbucks® for my Caramel Macchiato" to "I didn't come here to pray."

Most unsaved people don't have a natural appreciation for the things of God. They may be respectful, but they will usually try to avoid you as a believer—because when you share the gospel message, you create an atmosphere that is foreign to them and oftentimes uncomfortable. So, I have discovered that you don't need to ask someone if he's ready to make Jesus Christ his Savior and Lord. We've been taught to do that, but Jesus Himself said that the harvest is *ready right now* (John 4:35)!

Does that mean that 100 percent of the people you talk to will always pray the prayer to receive salvation? No, but it does mean that they're ready; Jesus said they were. He has already paid the ultimate price. He did it more than 2,000 years ago in His death, burial and resurrection. The work to purchase salvation for mankind has been done. All that's left is for mankind to receive that sacrificial act—and the Person of Jesus Christ who died to save them, and who *ever lives!*

Dealing With Various Scenarios — What If the Person Refuses To Pray?

I was in a grocery store, where I shared the gospel with a man, but he didn't want to pray. I said, "Pray this prayer after me." He responded,

"No, I'm not ready." I answered, "Sure you are. Jesus died for you over 2,000 years ago. He insisted he wasn't ready so, finally, I said, "All right. You're ready, but I understand. God bless you." I let him go. You can't force people to pray with you who simply don't want to pray. But on the other hand, we must not be too quick to leave them after we've shared with them. We must stand ready to reap! We must compel them through love. If we're sensitive to the leading of the Holy Spirit, we'll know when it's time to stop and say, "All right—God bless you." We just don't want to stop prematurely and miss the reaping of a soul for the harvest. Oftentimes, we miss God because we give up just short of bringing the person into the kingdom of God.

What If the Person Answers, 'I'm Already a Christian'?

When I use the "pocket card" in soul winning, following the question, "Do you go to church in the area?" if someone answers yes, I don't just walk away, saying, "Praise God, Brother (or Sister)!" In other words, I never assume someone's a Christian just because he says he attends church. And often, even if he/she says, "I'm a Christian," I continue asking questions to be certain. People have various definitions of "Christian," or what it means to be a Christian.

If you're witnessing to someone who says, "I go to such-and-such church," "I'm a Christian," or "I'm going to heaven when I die," that's not the time to stop and walk away. It's time to ask the right questions and wait for a scriptural reply.

One time, I took a team of reapers out to a certain city in Texas, and we saw a woman wearing a T-shirt that read: "Got Jesus?" This woman was wearing a chain around her neck with a big cross pendant on it. We were actually at a Christian rally, so most people would automatically assume this woman was saved.

I walked up to this woman and began to ask her the questions written on my pocket card. I got to the part where I asked, "If you were to die right now, where would you go?"

"Heaven," she immediately replied.

I asked her, "If God were to say to you, 'Why should I let you in?' how would you answer?"

She was silent for several seconds. Finally, she said, "Uh...I don't know."

This woman had a real respect for the Lord and the things of God, but had never actually been born again. I went over the verses from Romans with her and said, "Let's pray." She prayed with me and became born again!

More recently, I was in a large discount department store, and I asked a man who was stocking shelves, "If you died right now, where would you go?"

He was adamant: "To heaven, without a doubt!"

I said, "Awesome! Now let me ask you—if God were to ask you why He should allow you into heaven, how would you answer?"

He thought for a few seconds and finally said, "I don't really know." I went straight to the Scriptures. I didn't give him any of my ideas or thoughts. Nor did I ask his permission to tell him what the Word says. I went straight to the Word because the Word is power (Romans 1:16). After sharing those three simple verses from Romans—Romans 3:23, Romans 6:23 and Romans 10:13—I concluded by saying, "Pray this prayer with me."

I didn't ask, "Would you like to pray?" I wasn't going to give him the opportunity to say no. (By the way, all this took place in less than three minutes. I didn't distract him from his job by teaching him long passages from the Bible or debating with him. I simply shared a few scriptures and prayed. There's a place for mentoring and discipling new believers after we get them born again. While you're "reaping" them into the Kingdom is not the time for that.)

There are many reasons why people think they're going to heaven when they die, yet they're deceived. They've never received Jesus Christ as Savior and Lord. The following are just a few reasons many give for why they think they're going to heaven:

- "I'm basically a good person."

- "I do a lot of volunteer work and things to help other people."

- "I give to the poor."

- "God is good, so He would never send me to hell."

- "My mother [or grandmother, aunt or some other relative] is a Christian."

- "I've read the Bible from cover to cover."

- "I go to church."

- "I've never killed anyone."

Since Jesus is the Way, the Truth and the Life—and no one can go to the heavenly Father except by Him (John 14:6)—you can plainly see that they're believing a lie. Acts 4:12 says there is no other Name under heaven by which we can be saved. God doesn't *send* anyone to hell. The only sin that will send someone to hell is the sin of *their* refusal to accept Jesus as Savior. John 3:3 says, "...Unless one is born again, he cannot see the kingdom of God."

In soul winning, it's important not to debate people's beliefs or engage them in a long discussion about Scripture. Instead, simply direct them to the three primary scriptures I've named: Romans 3:23, Romans 6:23 and Romans 10:13. Some people don't even believe that hell exists. Don't argue this point, either. Your job is to share the simple truth—Romans 3:23, Romans 6:23 and Romans 10:13!

What If the Person Is Already a Believer?

When you're talking to a person who's genuinely saved—he'll tell you that Jesus died for his sins, and he has made Jesus his Savior and Lord, you can still pray with him using the following script. The idea behind evangelism is to leave the people with whom you come into contact in a better place spiritually than before you met them.

> _____, let me ask you a question. On a scale of one to five—"one" being lukewarm and "five" being hot, or totally sold out to God—how would you rate your walk with God? [IF THE PERSON SAYS ANYTHING OTHER THAN "FIVE," CONTINUE:] I want to pray a prayer with you to reaffirm your faith today. Just pray this after me: "Heavenly Father, I believe Jesus died on the cross for me and rose again [RESPONSE]. I affirm once again that I give You my life—spirit, soul and body. I want Jesus Christ to live big in my heart, and I want to be on fire for You. In Jesus' Name. Amen."

Most believers are pleased to pray that prayer and will thank you for taking the time to minister to them. However, every once in a while, you'll encounter a fellow believer who tries to engage you in a debate over doctrine, such as water baptism, the Baptism in the Holy Spirit, heaven, hell, etc.

How to Avoid Strife and Maintain a Powerful Witness

Don't ever allow yourself to be drawn into that kind of "discussion." It is designed to distract you from what God has sent you to do—to reap and to be a blessing. You can simply say to someone who wants to argue with you, "Bless you, Brother (or Sister)" and go on your way.

If you know anything about fishing, you know that there are times you get your lure caught on something in the water, such as a stump.

You could wrestle with it, but sometimes, the best thing to do is to cut your line, re-bait your hook and recast the line.

So, when you encounter someone who wants to argue, you must be able to recognize it as a distraction from the enemy so you can "cut your line" and not miss an important catch! There are "fish" all around you—souls who need to be saved—so you don't want to waste your time on a "stump" or on another obstacle designed to get you tangled up and distracted from what you were sent to do. You're a reaper, not a debater. When you understand that, and remain focused on your vision and calling, it will be easy to cut yourself away, or extract yourself, from these kinds of situations.

What If Someone Requests Prayer for Something Else?

The purpose of soul winning is to reap the harvest of people's souls in obedience to the Father—and with a motive of love for Him and compassion for humanity. So, when we go out on the streets to do one-on-one or even group evangelism, we're there to be a blessing to the unsaved and to the saved. We want to leave the people we meet in a better state, or condition, than when we found them.

When I'm out on the street, I usually say to people before I leave them, "Mark 16:18 says that those who believe will lay hands on the sick, and the sick will get well. Do you have any pain or symptoms in your body?" If they answer in the affirmative, I say, "Let me pray for you." If the person is a female, I ask a female member of my group to lay hands on her while I pray, or I'll lay my hand on her forehead and pray. Over the years, we have witnessed countless healings with many receiving instant relief from pain.

If you feel intimidated about praying for the sick, I encourage you to meditate on Mark 16:15-18, reading the passage in different translations. Then you'll be equipped and ready to pray a simple prayer for the sick, such as this one:

> Lord, I thank You for Your Word that says if we believe, we'll lay hands on the sick, and they'll get well! Thank You for healing _____, and that every pain is gone, in Jesus' Name. Thank You that he [or she] is recovering—getting well—right now. In Jesus' Name I pray. Amen."

Then, I always encourage the person to act on his faith by doing something he couldn't do before. For example, if the person had pain in his knee, I'd ask him to work his knee in a way that he may have struggled with before. In doing that, he is stepping out in simple faith on God's Word.

Prayer for the Baptism in the Holy Spirit

I've often been asked how often I pray with people on the streets to be baptized in the Holy Spirit with the evidence of speaking in other tongues (Acts 2:4). I do that as I'm led to do it, and that's how I instruct my teams.

To be filled with the Holy Spirit is a subsequent experience to the new birth. The new birth experience is when the Holy Spirit comes to indwell the new believer (John 14:17). As an Agent of the new birth, the Holy Spirit removes the old, sin nature from the person and gives him or her a new nature, the life and nature of God—*eternal life* (2 Corinthians 5:17). So a person must first be born again!

But, after a person receives Jesus Christ as Savior and Lord, there are times when we lead that person into the Baptism in the Holy Spirit, right then and there. At other times, we teach the Baptism in the Holy Spirit as a basic doctrine in classes for new believers we conduct in our local church (many churches conduct similar types of classes for new believers).

Also, when we meet someone who's already saved, and we pray for him or her to be on fire for God, we may include prayer for that experience.

I prayed this way for a pastor whom I met at a Christian conference.

Just as Paul asked the new believers at Ephesus (Acts 19:2), I asked this man, "Have you received the Holy Spirit since you believed?" In other words, I asked him, "Have you received the Baptism in the Holy Spirit since you first believed in Jesus Christ and became a Christian?"

In Acts 19:2, the Ephesian believers said, "We have not so much as heard whether there is a Holy Spirit." Paul had to explain the experience to them, and it says in verses 5-6, "When they heard this, they were baptized in the name of the Lord Jesus. And when Paul had laid hands on them, the Holy Spirit came upon them, and they spoke with tongues and prophesied."

This pastor had already heard about the Baptism in the Holy Spirit, so I simply shared a couple of verses with him on how to receive this experience. We prayed, and he was baptized in the Holy Spirit with the evidence of speaking in other tongues!

It's important to familiarize yourself with scriptures that explain the Baptism in the Holy Spirit so you can lead someone in prayer who desires to receive this gift of "power for witnessing"—power for sharing the gospel with others.[2]

What About Tracts?

Tracts can be a mixed blessing. On the one hand, handing out tracts puts something permanent from the Word of God in people's hands concerning salvation. On the other hand, they can cause some believers to feel as if they are an acceptable substitute for actually sharing the gospel message personally.

Our evangelism teams do both. We hand out tracts[2] *and* preach the gospel. Our teams use tracts as icebreakers as we approach people. We hand them a tract and begin asking the questions on the pocket card. For example, we'll say, "Hey, let me give you one of these," and we give

---

2 We use the tract entitled *You Are Loved*, which can be downloaded at rileystephenson.com.

them a tract. Then we'll say, "By the way, I'd like to ask you a couple of questions. Do you live in the area?" And then we ask them about their church attendance, their spiritual condition, and we share Romans 3:23, Romans 6:23 and Romans 10:13. And lastly, we pray with them.

Twelve Keys for Successful Evangelism

Following are 12 keys for maximizing your street-evangelism campaigns, as well as your one-on-one witnessing:

1. Don't Debate

As we've already seen, our job as reapers or "sent ones" into the harvest (Mark 16:15) is to reap a harvest of people's souls, not to debate with other religions or even other Christian denominations. Many believers feel it's their responsibility to "defend the Lord" when they're witnessing. But, our job is simply to give out His Word and to allow the Word to do the work. Remember, His Word is His power (Romans 1:16). Going beyond that by arguing and debating is a distraction and a time-waster and should be avoided. The enemy will try to use people— even other Christians—to stop what God wants to do. Don't ever allow strife and debate in your witnessing efforts.

2. Be Nice to Other Churches and Evangelistic Outreaches

In your evangelism outreaches, you'll likely encounter other churches doing similar outreaches, and some may not like or approve of the way you're doing it. There's no need to take offense. Offense is another distraction that can keep you from successfully fulfilling your commission to witness and evangelize.

One time, a member of another church was handed one of our *You Are Loved* tracts and complained about it. He approached me, saying, "Riley, did you write this?"

"Yes," I answered.

"Well, there's nothing here about repentance. This is just the bare nuts-and-bolts of getting saved."

"Praise God!" I responded. I wasn't going to get into a debate about how to convert someone to Christ. I know in my heart that I am giving out the simple Word of God that produces the power of God to get people saved.

The man persisted, "But you don't even say anything about sin." I simply said, "I believe the Lord might be telling you to write a tract." And I left it at that. He wanted a debate, but I wanted to get on with what God had called me to do. I wasn't going to debate him. I chose to be nice, instead.

You need to recognize that anytime a person starts doing something good, there will always be those standing by who will criticize. Just write that down somewhere and remember it, because it's true! To illustrate this fact, you may have tried a hundred different diets, but then, finally, you find one that works for you, and you start losing weight. Before long, someone comes along to tell you, "No, no, no. You have to do this and that, too, or it won't work"! You'd discovered a key, but then someone wanted to "mess with your success."

So, in evangelizing the lost, realize and recognize what you will inevitably find yourself up against, and be prepared. *Don't allow yourself to become distracted.* Be nice, and keep moving along the path God has for you. The following passage of Scripture provides great wisdom for keeping yourself focused when "naysayers" challenge you and try to frustrate your plans:

> Let your eyes look straight ahead, and your eyelids
> look right before you. Ponder the path of your feet,
> and let all your ways be established. Do not turn
> to the right or the left; remove your foot from evil
> (Proverbs 4:25-27).

3. Refuse to Receive Rejection Personally

I've had people actually yell at me for giving them a tract that contains the good news of the gospel and of their redemption in Christ! When that happens, I just realize that they're not rejecting me, they're rejecting the message because of the blindness of their hearts. I pray for them and leave that with the Lord.

If you saw someone driving on a road you knew had a bridge out—yet he missed the warning signs and continued driving toward a steep cliff—you would try to warn him, wouldn't you? You would wave your arms, make a lot of noise, and do whatever you could to get the driver's attention. Why? Because you know you could probably get him to stop if you could just get his attention. You know a person would have to be out of his mind to continue down that road if he knew the danger and destruction that awaited him.

Similarly, many are heading down a wrong path spiritually because they're unsaved. They haven't accepted Jesus Christ as Lord. And the god of this world has blinded their minds to the truth (2 Corinthians 4:4). But, that doesn't mean we're just to give up and quit. A person isn't thinking straight or seeing things clearly if he rejects the good news of the gospel. Yet the light of God's Word is his only hope for having his darkness penetrated with God's glorious light.

> For we do not wrestle against flesh and blood,
> but against principalities, against powers, against
> the rulers of the darkness of this age, against
> spiritual hosts of wickedness in the heavenly places
> (Ephesians 6:12).

We must always remember that our "fight" is not with human flesh but with the enemy who tries to influence human flesh. So, when someone comes against us as we're presenting the gospel, it's not really him coming against us as much as it is the enemy coming against the gospel.

So the person is not rejecting *you,* he's rejecting *Jesus.* He is being influenced by spiritual darkness.

4. Don't Stay Too Long in One Place

I rarely go to a place and ask for permission to be there. Usually, when you bring attention to yourself like that, it makes people nervous, and they'll say no. But, when you go to a place, "hang out" for 20-30 minutes, and then leave, you're not attracting attention to yourself. You can hand out tracts and witness at Walmart®, shopping malls and so forth, without making a scene.

We usually separate into small groups at a certain time, and then have everyone meet back at our cars or at the church bus, at a designated time—usually around one-half hour later. We never stay at one location for hours at a time.

5. Obey Civil Authorities

Wherever you're witnessing, if a policeman approaches you and says, "You can't do that here," don't argue. Simply say, "All right. God bless," and leave the area. Even if you have a legal right to be there, don't debate the issue. We must show respect for those in authority (Romans 13:1).

One time, we were witnessing on a college campus, and after about 20 minutes, four security guards showed up and said, "You can't do this here." I could tell they were nervous. They were expecting a response from us that they've probably received before from other groups that sometimes contend with authority.

We simply smiled and said to them, "OK, that's cool. We understand."

We started to leave, but one of them said, "Hold it! Wait a minute!" They had called for backup, and about that time, a couple of police cars pulled up and sort of barricaded us in by blocking the exits. It was almost like a scene in which a special-forces team descends on a group of terrorists. We just stood there, feeling shocked. I had my hands in my pockets. I had one hand on my phone, because I actually wanted to take a picture of all of this! Suddenly, an officer said to me, "Get your hands out of your pockets!"

Stunned, I raised both hands in the air like I was under arrest! Then he said, "No, get your hands down—just keep them out of your pockets."

Throughout this situation, we were totally friendly and cooperative. The officers asked for our driver's licenses to check us out. (The fact that none of us had any outstanding traffic tickets was probably a testimony in itself!)

Soon, they let us go, and they ended up being very nice. The security guards had sort of sounded an alarm and had made the situation out to be something serious. These responding police officers were just doing their jobs. We treated them respectfully, and they treated us respectfully. However, I never did get the photo I'd wanted! (We also learned that at that particular campus, we needed a permit to hand out fliers and talk to people—something we will obtain in advance before going back there in the future.)

So, if you attract the attention of authorities when witnessing, walk in love. Be gentle and friendly, not contentious and hard to deal with. And, obey them with a smile! You won't win anything by fighting with authorities, but you may win a convert by leaving a good testimony and being the right kind of witness for the Lord!

Also, never place tracts or church advertisements under windshield wiper blades in parking lots. They can be such a nuisance when you're already in your car before you notice the "litter" on your windshield. They could actually block the driver's vision when the car is started—or they could simply fall off the car and litter the parking lot, which is also a nuisance.

You don't want to give your church or your own personal witness a bad name by being inconsiderate and annoying people!

6. Don't Talk to Busy Employees

Common sense should dictate here, but sometimes we need to state the obvious just to keep people from making trouble for themselves unnecessarily. Let's say, for example, you're in a Starbucks®, and there are three people in line behind you. You're placing your order with the barista. That's not the time to start sharing the gospel with that person while she's busy and other customers are waiting. Doing that would be obnoxious.

On the other hand, if it's a slow night, and there's no one behind you in line, you could witness. I understand that people are working, and I am by no means encouraging you to distract them from their jobs. But, as I said before, you could do what's on the soul winning card in less than three minutes. That's about as long as having a casual conversation—but you're not making small talk; you're sharing words of eternal life!

When I'm talking to someone who's working on the job, if he will give me a minute or two, I'll use that opportunity to share the gospel. But if the person asks me not to talk to him while he's on the job, I won't do it. I won't force the issue. I never want to hurt someone's conscience or get him in trouble with his boss.

Another key in witnessing to employees is to call the person by name, if he or she is wearing a name tag. We all love to hear our names spoken out. So, take advantage of this truth when approaching an employee to share the gospel.

7. Be Friendly and Smile!

Have fun sharing the Word of God with others! After all, it's not you saving the person or doing the work. God's Word is His power, and *He* does the work, not you. Your only job is to share God's Word and pray. God will do the rest, transforming people's hearts from darkness to light!

Proverbs 18:24 says, "A man who has friends must himself be friendly...." People will not be open to you or your message if you are unfriendly toward them. So, determine to smile and allow the joy of Jesus to shine from your heart outward to others. Your joy will be contagious and difficult to resist!

8. Stick to the Card

I've already made reference to the pocket card, or the "soul winning card" we use in our evangelism outreaches. Whether you download it from my website and take it with you—which I recommend—or memorize it, it's important to stay with it and not allow yourself to become sidetracked from the simple words and scriptures on the card.

I have trained evangelism groups and overseen soul winning outreaches for more than 10 years, and I can tell you from personal experience that *less* really is *more!* You may be tempted to share your own testimony of salvation when you're witnessing—and God can certainly bless that at the right time—but His Word is the most anointed tool you have. And, you must be mindful to keep what you share very, very simple.

Because your spirit is alive to God as a believer, when you share His Word with others, you can almost feel the anointing to preach come on you! You have an audience, so the temptation may be great to start sharing other scriptures.

That's not wrong in itself, but to an unbeliever, hearing your testimony and scripture after scripture can feel overwhelming. So, take it from me, you will be more effective more often by simply "staying with the card"! After you get the person saved, you can take time, as you're led, to further share with him or her. That kind of sharing falls under the category of discipling or mentoring.

9. Leave Them With Something

As I said, we hand out tracts as we're witnessing to people so we can place something in their hands they can read later. I keep these tracts in my car and encourage team members to do the same—or in their purses or briefcases. Remember, tracts are not a substitute for sharing the good news, personally, and praying the prayer of salvation with others. Nevertheless, they are an important evangelism tool.

There will be times when you will not be able to share what's on the pocket card or pray with the person. For example, you might catch a businessperson on his or her way to a meeting. In a case like that, it's wonderful to be able to give the person a tract and say, "Read this when you get a chance."

On our tract, we list our church name, service times, contact information and a map to the church. There's also a portion that can be torn off, on which the person can write his or her name and contact information for follow-up, if the person prayed the prayer for salvation. You keep that portion, but the new convert gets to keep the tract for future reference. (We'll discuss the topic of follow-up in greater detail later.)

10. Trust God for Your Needs

Many believers become so distracted by anxieties, worries and the cares of life that they are rendered ineffective as reapers. But, there is a principle that if you'll put God and His kingdom first, He will take care of your needs (Matthew 6:33). So, rest assured, when you become involved with what interests God, He will involve Himself with your needs and concerns.

> But seek first the kingdom of God and His
> righteousness, and all these things shall be added to
> you (Matthew 6:33).

11. Don't Overuse Christian Jargon

When witnessing to the unsaved, it's important not to speak

"Christianese." In other words, using a lot of words that are familiar only in Christian circles, or using too many Christian "catch phrases" is almost like speaking a foreign language to them!

Remember, we saw that the natural man—the unsaved or unspiritual man—is unfamiliar with the things of God, or with the things of the Spirit. The unsaved have difficulty enough understanding or discerning these things without confusing them with words like "hallelujah," or "I'm saved and sanctified," or "I'm redeemed." But, the Spirit of God can minister life to them if we'll keep our message very simple and direct, delivering it with compassion instead of as a sermonette or in a "preachy" way.

12. Don't Make Promises You Can't or Are Not Willing to Keep

One time, we were witnessing in the downtown Fort Worth area, and a certain woman came out with us for the first time. She came across a homeless couple and had so much compassion toward them that she just blurted out, "I want to introduce you to Riley. He's going to get you some food tonight and arrange some transportation to church. And he will connect you with some housing."

When I met up with this woman, and she repeated what she had promised this husband and wife, I had to set her straight in front of the couple. I simply said, "I appreciate _____'s heart of compassion. Yes, I will feed you tonight. In fact, let's go right now and get you something to eat. But our church doesn't have a transportation program in place at this time, and the best I can do for you in terms of housing is to provide you with some contact information for a couple of local shelters I know about in this area."

I basically had to "undo" almost everything this very kind but misguided woman had said. But it's better to have integrity before people than to promise something you can't or are not willing to deliver. And, it's equally wrong to promise that *someone else* is going to make good on your promise if you haven't talked to that other person first!

We must be very careful how we handle the unsaved. We don't want to do or say anything that might color their view of God and the good news of the gospel, even if we mean well. We may be trying to impress them, but the simple truth always speaks volumes.

The *how-to* of soul winning is not complicated. In fact, the simpler we can keep things, the more effective we'll be at communicating the very simple truths from God's Word that will save and change people's lives. Using these 12 scriptural guidelines for witnessing, when we "keep it simple" and speak the truth in love, gives the Lord room to work His wonders in the hearts and lives of the people He came to save.

CHAPTER 3

THE POWER OF GOD'S WORD TO SAVE

"Are you saved?"

Y ou may have been asked this question at some point. If you weren't raised in a Christian home, perhaps you wondered, *Saved from what?* Or, maybe someone explained to you that salvation means, in essence, *being saved from the kingdom of darkness and translated into the Kingdom of light—God's kingdom.*

A person who's *saved* has been "reborn," his old nature has been removed, and he has been filled with the life of God. He has been saved from spiritual and eternal death, from hell and its eternal torments.

We hear the word *saved* mostly in the context of a "saved soul." But, really—to be scripturally accurate—we *are* a spirit, we *have* a soul and we *live in* a body (1 Thessalonians 5:23). The physical body is what we use to contact the physical realm in which we live. The soul is made up of the mind, will and emotions. With our souls, we contact the mental and intellectual realms. And with the spirit—the real man, or our inner man— is how we contact God. So, really, when we talk about soul winning, we're actually talking about getting people's *spirits* reborn or re-created in Christ (2 Corinthians 5:17).

We've already seen that God's Word is not just any word. It's not the word of man, but the Word of God that lives and abides forever (1 Peter 1:23). God's Word is His power. Power to do what? To do what it was sent to do—to cause faith to come (Romans 10:17), to cause fruit to be produced (Romans 6:22, 7:4), to change and transform (Romans 12:2).

Romans 10:17 says:

> **So then faith comes by hearing, and hearing by the word of God.**

Faith is of the heart, and with the heart, or spirit, is how we contact God. God is not a mind. We don't communicate with Him through our minds, reason or thought. God is a Spirit (John 4:24). We communicate with Him through our spirits, and it's through our spirits that He communicates with us.

Have you ever heard it said that God's Word, the Bible, is *God speaking to us?* It's true. God speaks to us through His Word. His Word is His will, and God and His Word are one (John 1:1-14).

What happens when someone hears the Word being taught, read, shared or proclaimed? It goes into his or her heart, and faith comes. Therefore, when you share Romans 3:23, Romans 6:23 and Romans 10:13 with someone, faith comes. Faith comes to understand and believe that all have sinned and that the wages of sin is death, but the gift of God is eternal life in Jesus. Faith comes to believe that whosoever calls on the Name of the Lord Jesus shall be saved (Romans 10:13).

Following are scriptures that show the living, transforming power of God's Word:

> **For the word of God is living and powerful, and sharper than any two-edged sword, piercing even to the division of soul and spirit, and of joints and**

marrow, and is a discerner of the thoughts and intents
of the heart (Hebrews 4:12).

So shall My word be that goes forth from My mouth;
It shall not return to Me void, but it shall accomplish
what I please, and it shall prosper in the thing for
which I sent it (Isaiah 55:11).

Then the Lord said to me, "You have seen well,
for I am watching over My word to perform it."
(Jeremiah 1:12. *NASB).*

The Lord said to me, "You have seen correctly, for
I am watching to see that my word is fulfilled"
(Jeremiah 1:12, *NIV).*

So the Word of God, the Scripture, is not just words! It is alive,
powerful, active, performing, fulfilling, productive and sharper than
any two-edged sword. It can distinguish between the soul and the spirit
of man and can discern the thoughts and intents of the heart. In other
words, God's Word will do what it is sent to do! It will do the job and
take care of business!

As reapers sent out into the harvest fields of the world—our neighborhoods, communities, cities, states and nations—we must never
underestimate the Spirit-inspired, Spirit-backed power of the gospel of
Jesus Christ, the *good news!*

For "whoever calls on the name of the Lord shall be
saved." How then shall they call on Him in whom
they have not believed? And how shall they believe
in Him of whom they have not heard? And how shall
they hear without a preacher? And how shall they
preach unless they are sent? As it is written: "How
beautiful are the feet of those who preach the gospel
of peace, who bring glad tidings of good things!" But

> they have not all obeyed the gospel. For Isaiah says,
> "Lord, who has believed our report?" So then faith
> comes by hearing, and hearing by the word of God
> (Romans 10:13-17).

Not only must we understand the power of the Word to do the work of transforming broken lives and rescuing those on their way to hell—we must also treasure the fact that the world is looking for us! They're looking for the Savior, and He's coming to them through us and our witness, through our obedience to the Great Commission. Verse 15 says, "How beautiful are the feet of those who preach the gospel of peace, who bring glad tidings of good things!"

Certainly, there will be those who reject the message. Verse 16 says, "But they have not all obeyed the gospel...." But, I guarantee that the deepest part of an unsaved person cries out for a Savior. He or she may be looking for "salvation" in drugs, alcohol, relationships, music, material possessions and other things that can only temporarily make him or her feel satisfied or "filled." But without Jesus, the internal void only God can fill, will remain vacant.

So, when you tell someone that Romans 3:23 says, "For all have sinned and fall short of the glory of God" and Romans 6:23 says, "For the wages of sin is death, but the gift of God is eternal life in Christ Jesus our Lord"; and when they hear "Whoever calls on the name of the Lord shall be saved," faith is instantly present in that person's heart to believe. When that new belief is acted on and the person prays the prayer of salvation with you, you will have reaped the harvest of another soul won for God's kingdom!

One reason I teach people to stay with the pocket card with these scriptures written on it, and to not get sidetracked quoting too many scriptures, is that once faith comes, it's important to get the person to act on his or her faith as quickly as possible. Don't ask if he is ready to pray because the eternal, unchanging, incorruptible seed of the Word of God was just "injected" into his spirit—and it will not return to God void (Isaiah 55:11)! So, even if the person refuses to pray and just walks away, the Word will continue to do its work in the heart.

Now you can see the importance of Isaiah 55:10-11. Let's look at it again:

> The rain and snow come down from the heavens and stay on the ground to water the earth. They cause the grain to grow, producing seed for the farmer and bread for the hungry. It is the same with my word. I send it out, and it always produces fruit. It will accomplish all I want it to, and it will prosper everywhere I send it (Isaiah 55:10-11, *NLT*).

Don't ever allow yourself to be discouraged if someone you've witnessed to refuses to pray. You just quoted three powerful verses from the living Word of God to that person—Romans 3:23, Romans 6:23 and Romans 10:13. God sent His Word out through you and, according to Isaiah 55:11, it *will* produce fruit in the lives of those who embrace it.

I heard a prominent minister testify one time that he was witnessing to a man—actually, all he did was quote Romans 10:13 to him: "Whoever calls on the name of the Lord shall be saved." The man didn't pray with the minister right then. But the very next day, he learned that the man later prayed the prayer of salvation, calling on the Name of the Lord, just as the scripture he heard had said!

When did faith come for this man to call on Jesus' Name? The day he acted on that verse? No, faith came the instant the minister quoted Romans 10:13 to the man.

The Word Does the Work—The Word Gets the Glory!

One time, while eating on the outdoor patio at a certain restaurant, four girls walked by me. The Lord said to me, *Talk to those girls about Me.*

I immediately said, "Hey, girls, I have something to share with you." Three of them kept walking, but one girl stopped. When I got to the part where I said, "If you died right now, do you know where you'd go?" she answered flatly, "I'd go to hell."

I shared Romans 3:23, Romans 6:23 and Romans 10:13 with her and said, "Let's pray." She prayed with me, asking Christ into her heart. Afterward, she said, "What are you trying to do—*save* me?" It was too late. She had gotten reborn before her flesh, or her natural man, knew what had happened!

I said, "Get your friends over here." They had been watching at a distance. The other girls walked over to us, and they too, ended up praying the prayer!

God's Word works!

A man shared with me an amazing testimony about the power of God's Word to transform a life. Here is his brief testimony:

> Forty days ago today, I told my girlfriend to stop trying to share Christ with me. I told her I am an atheist—that I would always be an atheist—and that I didn't want any of that "Jesus stuff." She persisted. "Just pray with me," she pleaded over and over. Finally, I prayed with her. Honestly, I did it just to shut her up. Then, I bluntly told her, "Now, leave me alone."
>
> Three days later, I came home from work and flipped on the TV to watch one of my favorite comedy shows because I wanted to laugh. But, that didn't really do it for me. So, I flipped over to a hockey game that was in overtime. That did nothing for me, either. Suddenly, I had such a desire to read a Bible! I turned off the TV and started reading the Bible!

When this man shared his testimony with me, I had just recently met him. The two of us had gone out witnessing—and he was barely a month old in the Lord! Praise God! His Word does not return void! No matter what people may say to you, and no matter how bad their case looks from a natural standpoint, God's Word is full of power, and *it works!*

After this man had prayed the prayer for salvation with his girl-friend and began reading the Bible, he got so fired up about the Lord that he began getting many people saved! He called me one day and said, "I got my doctor saved, and I just got my secretary saved!" This man was just a baby Christian, yet he was already a successful soul winner! Why? Was it because he had a special gift? No, his only gift was his own salvation and the Word of God coming out of his mouth as he shared the good news of Christ!

We Must Determine to Live by Faith in God's Word

Think about this for a moment: What if that man's girlfriend had just taken the attitude, *It's no use. I'm not going to share with him. He's an atheist, and he'll always be an atheist. He has made up his mind, and now he's going to hell!* Instead, her faith was set. She didn't give up, and today, they're happily married, living for God and still winning souls!

Many of us in the Body of Christ have been taught to walk by faith. We've been taught how to believe God for our needs and desires. But walking by faith is a *lifestyle.* The Bible says that the just, or righteous, shall *live* by faith (Habakkuk 2:4; Romans 1:17; Galatians 2:20, 3:11; Hebrews 10:38). So, whether we're believing for the answer to some need in our lives or standing in faith for the salvation of someone's soul, we must base our faith on the integrity of God's holy Word, not on what we see happening around us.

Numbers 23:19 says:

> God is not a man, that He should lie, Nor a son of man, that He should repent. Has He said, and will He not do? Or has He spoken, and will He not make it good?

The *NLT* says:

> God is not a man, that he should lie. He is not a
> human, that he should change his mind. Has he ever
> spoken and failed to act? Has he ever promised and
> not carried it through?

God is not a man; He's a Spirit (John 4:24). He has no capability of telling a lie. So what He says, He means! What He promises, He will perform! And, He can be depended on every time because He "changes not."

> For I am the Lord, I change not... (Malachi 3:6, *KJV*).

> Jesus Christ is the same yesterday, today, and forever
> (Hebrews 13:8).

Let's look at a few more verses that exalt the power, honor and integrity of God's Word:

> You have magnified Your word above all Your name
> (Psalm 138:2).

> Your promises are backed by all the honor of your
> name (Psalm 138:2, *NLT*).

> So the word of the Lord grew mightily and prevailed
> (Acts 19:20).

We've seen this verse several times, but it bears repeating here:

> I am not ashamed of this Good News about Christ.
> It is the power of God at work, saving everyone who
> believes... (Romans 1:16, *NLT*).

The Good News is the gospel, or the Word of God. And God's

Word is His power. It's not my opinion—or yours—that produces God's manifested power. It's not rules or regulations. No, it's the Word of God: the Good News of Jesus Christ.

We Need the Word, But the Word Needs Us, Too

Certainly, God's Word is self-sustaining and contains within it the power to reproduce itself and to bear fruit. But, we also read Romans 10:14-15, which says, "How then shall they call on Him in whom they have not believed? And how shall they believe in Him of whom they have not heard? And how shall they hear without a preacher? And how shall they preach unless they are sent? As it is written: 'How beautiful are the feet of those who preach the gospel of peace, who bring glad tidings of good things!'"

In other words, the Word will do the work, but it must be preached or proclaimed. That's where believers come in. We've been commissioned—*sent*—to reap the harvest of souls from the "fields" that Jesus said were white or ready for harvest (see Mark 16:15-18; John 4:35).

Many of us in the Body of Christ have been taught to walk by faith to receive our needs and desires met—to receive the provisions of God's promises and our redemption in Christ. We understand that "we walk by faith, not by sight" (2 Corinthians 5:7). We've been taught that we're to trust in the integrity of God and His Word, no matter how things look or how we think or feel.

The same is true when we're trusting God's Word to work for the reaping of a harvest of souls. I have experienced this truth many, many times. There have been times when I just didn't feel like sharing, but when I did it anyway, the Word worked its wonders, and souls were saved—translated from darkness to light!

I'll share an example along those lines that really had an impact on me. My wife and I had purchased an investment property, and I was at the property late one night painting it for resale. I finished the job and, on the way home, was so sleepy, I stopped at a convenience store for a cup of coffee just so I could make it home without falling asleep at the wheel. I had been perspiring and was covered with paint over-spray. I was wearing a baseball cap and painting clothes, and had spatters of paint all over my face. As I was paying for my coffee, I noticed my pocket card in my billfold (in those days, I printed them smaller in size—about the size of a business card). As I looked at the card, I sensed the Lord saying, *Tell this clerk about Me.*

My first reaction was not one of eager obedience and enthusiasm! In fact, I said inwardly, *I don't want to do this right now.* But without giving my flesh time to talk me out of it, I opened my mouth and said, "Hi, ma'am. How are you tonight?"

When I got to the part on the pocket card that says, "If you died right now, where would you go?" she said, "I'd go to hell."

"Well, let me share with you what the Bible says," I answered, and I gave her the salvation message in three easy scriptures—Romans 3:23, Romans 6:23 and Romans 10:13!

I felt so "out of it" and ready to go home, shower and get some sleep that I wasn't even looking at her; I was reading straight from the card in a sort of monotone voice.

I said, "Now, pray this prayer with me." I was standing there in front of her—stinky, dirty and sweaty—but she repeated the words of that prayer, nevertheless, and got saved at that moment!

As I thought about it later, I had to marvel at the power of the glorious gospel of Christ! So often when we lead someone to Christ, we think it's because we're especially anointed or because our presentation was so well delivered. But, it's the Word of God that's anointed! The Word is the power! This was never more true than on that night, as I stood before that woman simply reading the salvation message to her from a business card!

Another amazing thing about that encounter was, when I asked her name, she said, "Marianna." *I was stunned.* My mother, who'd gone on to heaven several years previously, was named Marianna. That's not a name you hear every day, and it was like music to my ears to hear it that night. It's just like the Lord to bless us when we're taking care of His business!

From the Mouths of Babes

We know that the Word of God is the power of God and that it can change any person, situation or circumstance. As long as we use the Word, keeping it in our hearts and mouths (Romans 10:8), as we have seen, it will not "return void" (Isaiah 55:11). It will produce fruit and accomplish what it was designed to do! This is true no matter how old or young we are—or whether we've been saved for one day or 50 years! When we understand the power resident in the Word of God, we take the pressure off ourselves to witness because we know that it's the Word doing the work, not us.

I know a little girl who began witnessing, using the pocket card when she was just 7 years old! She would walk up to people and start reading. And, she'd lead people to Jesus! There aren't too many people who won't listen to a sweet, little child. As they'd listen, the Word would work on them, and they'd get saved!

So God meant what He said through the Apostle Paul in Romans 1:16: "For I am not ashamed of the gospel of Christ, for it is the power of God to salvation for EVERYONE who believes, for the Jew first and also for the Greek." And, Galatians 3:28 says, "There is neither Jew nor Greek, there is neither slave nor free, there is neither male nor female; for you are all one in Christ Jesus." We could also add that "in Christ," there is neither young nor old! We are all one *in Him.*

The Word and the Spirit Work Together— Count on the Holy Spirit to Help You!

One time, I was walking past a theater in downtown Fort Worth, and a man walked toward me dressed in a fancy suit with his hat cocked to one side. He was covered with sparkling jewelry and walked as if he didn't have a care in the world. I stopped him and said, "Hey, man, let me ask you a few questions."

Right away, he waved me off. "I don't want any of that stuff," he said, as if he knew what I was going to say. At that very moment, the Lord spoke to my spirit and said, *He might as well get saved. His granny has been praying for him every day.*

So I said to the man, "Dude, you might as well get saved. Your granny's been praying for you every day."

Stunned, the man said, "How do you know my granny?!"

I answered, "I don't know your granny. The Lord does, and He said to me, *He might as well get saved. His granny has been praying for him every day.*"

"OK," he said. "Let's pray."

Quickly, I shared with him "the three scriptures." After he prayed, I said, "Let's call Granny and tell her what happened."

He dialed his granny's number, and when she answered, he exclaimed, "Granny—I just met a guy who prayed with me to receive Jesus! Have you been praying for me?"

"Every day," she answered. The man looked at me shocked and amazed, like he'd seen a ghost.

I said, "Don't look at *me,* dude—this is all Jesus."

If you'll read the Great Commission in Mark 16, you'll notice that after it says, "Go," it says, "And they went...and preached every where, the Lord working with them and confirming the word with signs following" (verse 20, *KJV*). God will use all His resources to get people born again. He will give you signs—words of knowledge, words of wisdom, and words of prophecy—whatever it takes to get the job done.

So, expect that! You are no less equipped than the disciples of the early Church. When God says, *"Go!"* you can rest assured He will go with you! All He asks is that you speak out His Word. He'll do the work.

Reapers Are 'Opportunists' With a Message!

The Word of God is always full of power and is "front and center"—always ready to work on behalf of those who receive it. We should look for every opportunity to proclaim it. God wants us to be ready and on *go* where His Word and salvation message are concerned.

A couple of years ago, I was shopping with my teenage daughter at a mall, and we walked up to a kiosk that sold sunglasses. There was a sign that read, "Two for $19.99." I told my daughter, "Go pick out some sunglasses." My daughter is a "daddy's girl," and I certainly wanted to buy her those sunglasses. But, my real motive was to gain an opportunity to minister the gospel to a lost soul. We were the only customers at the kiosk, so as my daughter shopped for sunglasses, I presented the simple gospel message to the clerk.

The woman said, "Oh, no—I don't want to hear that. I'm a Buddhist."

Just as the pocket card instructs, I didn't argue. Instead, I simply said, "Awesome." Then I felt impressed to get this woman a Bible, so I said to her, "I'm going to go and buy you a Bible. I'll be right back." We paid for our sunglasses and left.

Soon, I was back with a brand-new Bible. I presented it to this woman, and she was floored. She stared at me, surprised, as if she were thinking, *Man, this guy actually did what he said he would do.*

That's one reason I emphasize not over-promising things when you're witnessing to others. People are watching to see if you're going to keep your word or not. So, don't tell someone you're going to pick him up for church on Sunday if you're not willing to follow through and give him a ride to church.

As this woman at the sunglasses kiosk took the Bible from my hands, she asked, "Do you know where a person can go to get healing?"

I knew what she was talking about, but asked her, "What do you mean?"

All this woman knew of Christianity was what she'd seen on television or in movies. She was talking about "stigmata"—in this case, places where oil or what appeared to be blood oozed from certain statues or monuments, and people claimed to receive divine healing by touching or looking upon such objects.

Pointing to her new Bible, I told the woman, "We don't go anywhere for healing except here." I opened it to Mark 16:15-20. Then I said, "If this truly is the Word of God, you can receive healing right now because it says here when believers lay hands on the sick, they shall recover. It says that miraculous signs shall follow those who believe because they're proclaiming God's Word. And, God always works in line with His Word."

I continued, "I'm a believer. What's your trouble?"

She said, "My back really hurts."

"OK," I replied. "If this is truly the Word of God, when I place my hand on your back, you'll be healed. You'll begin to recover right now."

"OK," she said.

I asked her to place her hand on her own back, and I laid my hand on hers and prayed: "Lord, Your Word says that if we believe, we'll lay hands on the sick, and they'll get well. I thank You, Lord, that You take the pain away from her back, in Jesus' Name."

That's all I said. I didn't do any specific binding or loosing. I didn't shout. I didn't pray in tongues. I didn't pray in "Christianese"—in a way that this woman wouldn't even understand. I kept it simple, praying a simple prayer of simple faith in God's Word.

Suddenly, the woman exclaimed, "How did you do that? The pain is gone!"

"That's Jesus," I told her. Then I said, "Let me share three scriptures with you...." I shared Romans 3:23, Romans 6:23 and Romans 10:13—and the woman prayed to receive Jesus as Savior!

That was two years ago, and she still works at that sunglasses kiosk at the mall. Every time I'm there, I go by and visit with her. And, she's still doing great in the Lord!

Someone asked me, "Does she go to your church, now?" No, and she'll probably never attend our church. She lives more than 30 miles away, and there are other good churches in her area where she can get involved.

The point is, all I did was to pray a simple prayer, acting in simple faith in God's Word. I didn't try to make a scene or be dramatic. I didn't try to conjure something up on my own. I didn't have to. The Word did the work, as it will every time we're confident and bold enough to speak it forth and act on it in faith.

CHAPTER 4

DISCIPLESHIP AFTER THE DECISION—HOW TO FOLLOW UP WITH NEW BELIEVERS

One of the questions I'm most often asked regarding evangelism training is how to follow up with people once we pray with them to receive Christ.

Follow-up is critically important, and we have not neglected this facet of reaping the harvest. We use a follow-up tract entitled *You Made the Right Choice!* which can also be downloaded from my website. In this tract, there's space to take the new convert's name and contact information so that follow-up may be made by the host church or church in that area. We keep that part of the tract and leave the new believer with the remainder, which contains instruction and information from the Bible for the convert's walk with God.

Sometimes, new converts are leery about giving out their personal information, and that's OK. First, we assure them the church will not "hound" them, but will simply follow up by phone and perhaps send a letter. If written correspondence is sent, new believers may also receive additional materials to help them in their spiritual walk. (It's important to receive the correct follow-up information from your local church *before* you go out witnessing so that you don't make promises that you or someone else can't keep.)

Certainly, at the time of follow-up, new converts will be invited to attend the local church. It's important that all believers find a church they can call their "home church," where they can sit under the leadership of a godly, Bible-believing pastor and the teaching of the life-changing Word of God.

Some groups don't use a follow-up tract. They simply use information cards, take down the contact information, and send the new believer a tract or booklet by mail, along with an invitation to attend the church. Whichever you choose, it's important not to try to force new converts to provide you with their contact information.

When we encounter someone who doesn't wish to receive follow-up, we simply leave the entire tract and ask the person to mail his information to the church. The church name and contact information can be stamped on the back for his or her convenience. Whether we take the contact information back to the church or ask the convert to mail the information, we try to connect the new believer to a local church so discipleship can be initiated and the new believer can be integrated into a family of believers.

Some churches design their own follow-up packets to distribute to new believers, which often contain a map to the church and all the Web, mail or phone contact information needed. The important thing is that we make an attempt to connect new believers with a local church so they can grow in their newfound faith in Christ.

As a rule, we don't do any discipleship training on the streets. As

I said previously, we are far more effective if we move quickly. Street witnessing doesn't provide the proper venue for teaching and training, but *is* an excellent venue for proclaiming the simple gospel message. We share the three scriptures, pray, receive contact information and go on to the next soul in that harvest field. Some Christians don't approve, but this method has been extremely effective for us for many years.

It's important to do your part in the harvest, and then give God room to work in the hearts and lives of new believers. You can't force an individual to be saved, nor can you force them to go to church, give you their contact information or make them contact the church. But there *are* vast numbers of people in the world who *will* respond and cooperate with the process of becoming discipled and trained as new believers. Our time must be spent on those people—and pray for those we, sadly, have to leave behind.

What *Is* Follow-Up, Anyway?

Many of us have come to think of follow-up as praying with someone to receive Jesus Christ as Savior, buying the person a giant Bible and concordance, and then showing up at his house once a week to show him how to do word searches in the Hebrew and Greek! We think we have to take him to the Christian bookstore and load him down with Christian books, jewelry, T-shirts and tickets to the next Christian concert. After that, we inform the person that he must get rid of all his secular music so we can effectively pump him full of the Word!

That's total overkill—and doing all those things at such a fast pace could be confusing to a new believer instead of blessing and encouraging him. Certainly, we don't want to leave him ignorant of God's Word, but we don't want to overwhelm him, either!

Follow-up is about establishing relationships and loving the new believer, letting him know that not only is he accepted by God, but by God's family. Ephesians 1:6 says, "To the praise of the glory of His grace, by which He made us *accepted in the Beloved.*"

Many churches I've had the privilege of working with through the years, have excellent follow-up programs that include new-believers classes held on-site at the church each Sunday just before the main service. People in the church are assigned to call on the new convert, pray with him, answer any questions he might have and work to guide that person into a fulfilling life of spiritual growth and service among a loving family of believers.

Don't Judge the New Believer

Some Christians can be very critical of the "young in Christ," and it is disturbing. For instance, someone said to me one time, "Riley, today I saw a guy that we led to the Lord last night, and he was smoking a cigarette and drinking a beer."

We aren't to judge fellow believers—the Bible commands us not to do it (Romans 2:1). Judging, if it is necessary, belongs to God, and to Him alone. When a person receives Jesus as his Savior, he is born again of incorruptible seed—the Word of God that lives and abides *forever* (1 Peter 1:23). It's really not our place to second-guess the inner working of God's incorruptible Word in another person's life. And, remember, God's Word doesn't return void, but it ultimately accomplishes everything it was sent to do when embraced by the recipient.

Ephesians 4:30, *(NLT)*, says:

> **Remember, he has identified you as his own, guaranteeing that you will be saved on the day of redemption.**

When God identifies someone as His own, He guarantees he or she will be saved "on the day of redemption" when Jesus returns for His Church and separates the "tares from the wheat" (Matthew 13:30). I didn't write that—God Himself inspired it. It's His holy Word!

Just How Saved *Are* They?

When we accept Christ and His sacrifice at Calvary, we become thoroughly born again. We are immediately baptized into Christ (Galatians 3:27). But, each of us walks out our redemption and salvation as we grow in Him, and each grows by degree—just as a child physically grows and develops from infancy to toddler, youth, adolescent and finally, a full-grown adult.

Our job is not to monitor and examine a new believer's fruit, but to teach and train him in the Word of God. Then, we must trust the Holy Spirit to work in the life of that brother or sister in Christ. The Holy Spirit is the ultimate Teacher and Trainer (John 16:13; 1 John 2:20, 27). He is the best "Follow-Upper" on the planet!

Establishing the New Believer in the Father's Love

Teaching the Word of God will either establish new beliefs in a person's life or strengthen existing beliefs. Following are some scriptures to use in follow-up and discipleship training to teach and strengthen the new believer in Christ:

> All whom My Father gives (entrusts) to Me will come to Me; and the one who comes to Me I will most certainly not cast out [I will never, no never, reject one of them who comes to Me]. For I have come down from heaven not to do My own will and purpose but to do the will and purpose of Him Who sent Me. And this is the will of Him Who sent Me, that I should not lose any of all that He has given Me, but that I should give new life and raise [them all] up at the last day. For this is My Father's will and His purpose, that everyone who sees the Son and believes in and cleaves to and trusts in and relies on Him should have eternal life, and I will raise him up [from the dead] at the last day (John 6:37-40, *AMP*).

> And I give them eternal life, and they shall never lose
> it or perish throughout the ages. [To all eternity they
> shall never by any means be destroyed.] And no one
> is able to snatch them out of My hand. My Father, Who
> has given them to Me, is greater and mightier than all
> [else]; and no one is able to snatch [them] out of the
> Father's hand (John 10:28-29, *AMP).*

Isn't that awesome? The Bible says that when we win souls, we snatch them from the flames of judgment (Jude 23), but these scriptures also show that once they're saved, no one is able to snatch them out of the Father's hands.

Just before His crucifixion, while praying in the Garden of Gethsemane, Jesus said to the Father, "Of those whom You gave Me I have lost none" (John 18:9). When a person is born again, he is stamped with the seal of the Holy Spirit. In other words, his life is "branded" by God, who eternally secures the lives of those who are His own.

Ephesians 1:13-14 says:

> In Him, you also who have heard the Word of Truth,
> the glad tidings (Gospel) of your salvation, and have
> believed in and adhered to and relied on Him, *were*
> *stamped with the seal of the long-promised Holy*
> *Spirit.* That [Spirit] is the guarantee of our inheritance
> [the firstfruits, the pledge and foretaste, the down
> payment on our heritage], in anticipation of its full
> redemption and our acquiring [complete] possession
> of it—to the praise of His glory *(AMP).*

And, chapter 4:30 says:

> And do not grieve the Holy Spirit of God [do not offend
> or vex or sadden Him], by Whom *you were sealed*
> *(marked, branded as God's own,* secured) for the day

of redemption (of final deliverance through Christ from
evil and the consequences of sin) *(AMP).*

Now, let's look at a verse that talks about the Christian's name being
written in the "Lamb's Book of Life" (Revelation 21:27):

And I [Paul] urge you also, true companion, help
these women who labored with me in the gospel,
with Clement also, and the rest of my fellow workers,
whose names are in the Book of Life (Philippians 4:3).

"Can their names be erased once they're written in that precious
book?" someone may ask. What God has written, He has written—and
it isn't up to us or anyone else to judge where someone is or isn't going
when he leaves this earth.

Many people know John 3:16 says: "For God so loved the world
that He gave His only begotten Son, that whoever believes in Him
should not perish but have everlasting life."

Not nearly as many can quote the next verse:

For God did not send His Son into the world to
condemn the world, but that the world through Him
might be saved (verse 17).

Since Jesus didn't come to condemn the world, but to save it, we're
not to condemn people, either. Our job is to preach the good news.
The Lord does the work in causing a person to be born again. And, in
the same way, once a person receives Him as Savior and Lord, the Lord
does the work of growing that person up in Him. We can disciple or
teach and train new believers, but ultimately it's the Lord who gives the
increase and brings forth His Word in their lives as they submit themselves to it. The Word transforms them from the inside out.

Once we introduce someone to Jesus and distribute the follow-up tract or card, we know we've done what we can do. The local church or Christian organization will then follow up on the new believer, if at all possible, and God will be glorified in it all.

Disciples Are Willing Participants in the Gospel

People have said to me, "Riley, we need more *disciples,* not more *decisions."* And they refer to Matthew 28:19, which says, "Go therefore and make disciples of all the nations, baptizing them in the name of the Father and of the Son and of the Holy Spirit."

I always tell those people, "I can't *make* a disciple. Neither can you. I can lead people into an environment where they can be mentored, taught and trained. But I can't *force* people to become disciples, no matter how many times I call them, write to them or visit them."

A disciple is *a committed learner or follower.* Discipleship implies a decision has been made on the part of the one being discipled. A willful commitment is required. He will connect to a church or ministry by choice, not because of being coerced or constantly called and pursued by a church or organization.

For example, Jesus' original 12 disciples followed Him by choice. He chose them, but they had to *choose to follow Him.* He said, "Follow Me, and I will make you fishers of men" (Matthew 4:19). Jesus didn't constantly pursue them, He invited them, and as a result, they committed themselves to Him and followed Him.

Not everyone followed Jesus when He invited them. In Matthew 8:21, a man said that he'd follow the Lord, but hesitated, saying, "Lord, let me first go and bury my father." Jesus responded, "Follow Me, and let the dead bury their own dead" (verse 22).

This is true of so many people today. They want to follow, but they have this, that and the other thing they want to do first. In other words, they haven't committed themselves. And no matter what you do, you can't commit *for* these people—and you can't *make* them commit.

I can definitely say I'm a disciple of my pastors because I chose to be, not because they called me every week. I chose to connect with my church and pursued the connection—in much the same way I imagine the disciples pursued their connection with Jesus.

There are many who pursue a connection with my ministry, not because I follow up on them constantly or because I'm constantly pursuing them. I'm teaching them to do what I do. I'm mentoring and training them, but it's not because I chase them down to get the job done! No, they choose to connect themselves with my ministry and to learn from me. Certainly, I follow up on them. In fact, I often call those who are now leading their own outreaches to see how they're doing. But, I don't force people to become involved with my ministry or to go out and lead ministries of their own.

God calls individuals to certain churches to fulfill a certain purpose. But, when God calls you, that means you must answer. He won't drag you into church—and neither will I! But He will urge, woo and prompt you in the direction of His choosing. How you respond determines the level of teaching and training you'll be able to receive.

CHAPTER 5

SETTING 'SOUL GOALS'

I t's a well-known fact that successful people succeed in life because *they make plans to succeed.* In other words, most success stories we hear or read about didn't happen by accident. They happened because someone had a desire and set a goal to succeed.

A good illustration would be in writing a budget or setting a goal to earn a certain amount of money by year's end. Your plan is to give more to a church or ministry, go on a vacation, buy an automobile, large appliance or make some kind of investment. If you've noticed, there's something about "writing the vision" (Habakkuk 2:2) that makes it more real and sets you on a clear path so you'll always know where you're going. Somehow, when it's written down, it isn't as easy to get sidetracked from achieving your goal. And, when you know what God's Word says about it—His will concerning your situation—you can be confident you'll succeed in achieving your goal.

What about God's will for the harvest? We've looked in-depth at His Word concerning His will and desire that souls be saved. Therefore, it's important to "write your vision" concerning how many souls you'd like to personally see saved over the course of a year or a set period of time.

Goals are so important in life. It's the will of God that we grow and improve in every area of our lives so that we never become stagnant. The Lord wants us to do better, to have more, and to go deeper in our spiritual walk. We're either moving forward and making progress or we're moving backward. The enemy of growth is apathy, and this is the very thing that causes people to be depressed. With no vision for their lives, people often get into trouble (Proverbs 29:18).

Maintaining an Eternal Perspective

Although goal setting is very important to our success and feelings of well-being in life, the only real success we can take with us when we die is our spiritual rewards that stem from our obedience to God's Word. You've, no doubt, heard the saying about money: "You can't take it with you." But, you *can* take with you the souls you've led to the Lord! The salvation of people's souls is spiritual substance that will endure forever. I once heard a preacher say something years ago that has stayed with me and marked me for life: "The only thing that matters when you die is what you've done for Jesus." Though it's commendable to set goals to earn more money, for example, that won't really matter where eternity is concerned. The streets of heaven are made of pure gold. God is not impressed by our houses, cars or other material possessions. But, He *is* impressed by our obedience to Him and the respect we show toward the things that matter to Him.

Startling Statistics

I recently read a statistic that globally, every second, approximately 1.78 people die. If this statistic is accurate, that means nearly 107 people die per minute, 6400 people per hour—and *almost 154,000 people every day!*

Doing the math, if these statistics are correct, that means that more than 56,000,000 people die every year. If a person lived to be 70 years old, then over his or her lifetime, approximately 3.9 billion people will have passed from this earth!

Based on those figures and the population of the world today, if you were to line up 1,000 people, theoretically, 10 would die within a year.

I don't base my life on statistics, and neither should you, but I am simply making you aware that physical death, as well as *spiritual* death, is a reality.

This is something many believers don't want to think about. But we must be conscious of the fact that when we pass people on the street, in the mall or in the grocery store, those people will slip from this earth into eternity one day. They will spend "forever" either in heaven or in hell. I don't know about you, but that motivates me to set some definite goals concerning how many people I want to lead to the Lord so that they can spend eternity with Him!

It's All About the Numbers

Some people have said to me, "It's not about the numbers, Riley. We shouldn't be so focused on numbers when it comes to ministering to people." But numbers *are* important. Ask any accountant, architect, engineer, physician or physicist—he or she will tell you that numbers are very, *very* important!

Throughout the Word of God, we can see that God is also interested in numbers. He gave Noah instructions to build the Ark that included precise measurements for the successful constructing of that impenetrable vessel of safety—a vessel that would secure Noah and his family, and every species of animal on the earth, against the complete devastation and destruction that was to come.

When God later gave instruction concerning the building of His temple, He again gave precise measurements that were to be used—*numbers*. In our everyday lives, whether we're talking about our family's finances or simply the number of calories we burn in a workout, it really is "all about the numbers."[1]

When I hear someone talk about the number of souls who came to Jesus during a particular outreach, I get excited. Whether it's 5, 25 or 2500, I like to hear about numbers because I see each outreach as an expansion of God's kingdom. And, before I die, I personally want to see as many people come to Jesus as possible. I'm not putting notches in my "gospel belt," but simply obeying the Word of God and His plans by taking my place to bring in the harvest!

And if there *were* such a thing as a gospel belt, I'd definitely want mine "notched up"—wouldn't you? So, don't ever allow a religious spirit to accuse you about winning souls. That spirit comes against believers who want to do something for God, so you're in good company if someone ridicules you for witnessing about Jesus!

How to Set Your 'Soul Goals'

Just as we set short and long-term goals for natural things like finances and acquiring of material things, we can set short and long-term 'soul goals.' For example, if you know you're going to participate in a street campaign for one night, set a 'soul goal' for yourself or your group for that particular night. If the group leader says he or she is believing God for 300 souls, and there are 10 groups going out that night, you could set a soul goal of 30 for your group.

If you're going to be out witnessing and handing out tracts for three hours that night, that would mean winning 10 people per hour to the Lord. Considering that you only spend a few minutes with each person

---

1 Read more about this topic in Riley's book *It's All About the Numbers* (Riley Stephenson: Newark, TX, 2009).

you approach, this is a very reasonable goal, especially since you'll often encounter people in pairs or small groups. Frequently, everyone in the group will pray the prayer of salvation with you.

Another way to set a soul goal is to ask the Lord's help in giving you a goal or a number He wants you to reach for that particular outing. Write down the number He impresses you with, and keep that vision or goal before you as you pray about the outreach. I've seen people do this many times. When God gives them a number, they always reach that goal—and often go beyond it. There's great joy in co-laboring with the Lord in reaching others for Him!

You Can Set a Goal by Simply Making Up Your Mind!

You don't always need a leader to help you set group goals. And, you don't always need to pray for God to give you a goal number of souls to reach. One time, a teenage girl participated in one of our street-witnessing campaigns. Before we went out, I had set a goal of 25 souls for each group. On the way to our destination, she made up her mind, *I'm going for a hundred!*

This young girl started calling people on her mobile phone and witnessing to them about the Lord. Then she worked hard on the streets all day. At the end of the day, she had led 100 people to the Lord! She reached her goal because she made up her mind and determined in her heart that she was going to do it—*and she did!*

Remember to Pray for Favor

As you're praying in preparation to witness, remember to ask God for supernatural favor (Psalm 5:12). Believe that the Lord will open doors for you to speak to those He has planned for you to meet, and believe that He'll give you opportunities to speak to large numbers of people.

The Lord has supernaturally opened doors for me to witness to bus-loads of people all at once—as well as to restaurants full of people.

"How do you handle that, Riley?" someone asked.

The first thing I do to get the attention of the whole crowd is to say, "I'm going to say a quick prayer over all of you tonight." Then, I begin praying: "Lord, bless everyone here. Bless them spirit, soul and body. Bless them in their health and in their finances. Lord, I thank You that Your Word says that all have sinned and come short of Your glory (Romans 3:23). And Your Word says that the wages of sin is death, but that the gift of God is eternal life through Jesus Christ, Your Son (Romans 6:23). Your Word also says that whosoever shall call upon the Name of the Lord shall be saved (Romans 10:13)."

Then I say: "If you're not 100 percent sure today that if you died, you'd go to heaven, pray this prayer after me. In fact, let's all pray the prayer." Then I ask everyone to repeat my prayer.

Lastly, I ask for a show of hands of everyone who prayed the prayer to accept Jesus. I count the number of hands and distribute the *You Made the Right Choice!* follow-up tracts to each one who prayed.

So, believe God for favor and then be bold enough to step out, confident that you've received. What's the worst thing that can happen? The bus driver or person in charge can say no and refuse to give you an audience. When that happens, you simply go to the next bus, restaurant, crowd or individual. God will give you uncommon, extraordinary favor and open many doors for you if you're using His favor to preach the gospel.

Pray, and Be Led

As I said previously, you don't have to pray to be led to witness to people because the Bible has already made clear God's will that we share the gospel—the good news. But, we can be led by the Spirit as we step out to do evangelism.

When I conduct Friday night evangelism-training sessions, we usually go out to a mall or to a Walmart® to witness after we're finished with the teaching portion. However, sometimes, we'll be impressed to go to another location. One time, I was impressed by the Lord to go to a large Mexican restaurant chain. It was one of those places where you raise the flag at your table when you want the waiter to bring you something.

I found the manager and said, "I'd like to say a quick prayer over everyone in this section."

She said, "Go ahead, I don't care."

There were about 10 or 15 people in that particular section. I didn't scream, but I spoke loudly enough for all of them to hear me. I said, "Hey, everyone, I just want you to know that God loves you and that He has a wonderful plan for your life." I shared Romans 3:23, Romans 6:23 and Romans 10:13. I said, "Let's pray."

Afterward, that same manager approached me and said, "I've heard that message before, but I have never prayed that prayer until tonight."

I asked her, "May I speak to your workers?"

She led me into the back of the restaurant, where there was a busy group of dishwashers. Quickly, I shared my simple message and led them in a prayer to receive Jesus!

I've done this very thing in a bingo hall. I approached the manager, told him I was a minister, and gave him my business card. He said, "Sure, you can pray. Just wait till we're done with this game."

When they finished that game, the manager handed me the microphone. I simply said, "Hey, everyone. I'm Riley, a minister from a local church, here. I want to pray a quick prayer over you guys, but first I want to share three scriptures...."

After I prayed the prayer of salvation, the Holy Spirit prompted me to pray for the sick. So I said, "If you need healing, lay your hand on that part of your body while I pray." Many people in that place laid their hands on their bodies—on their stomachs, backs, shoulders, knees and heads—and prayed with me.

When we walked out of that bingo hall that night, you would have thought we were movie stars! People waved, cheered, clapped, and yelled out, "God bless you! Thank you! Good night!"

What happened? Were we that cool? Were we dressed so stylishly that the people held us in admiration? No! It was the favor of God. He has done this for me time, and time again. And, if you will set a soul goal and believe God for favor, I guarantee, He will "show up" to guide and bless you and minister His life-changing power to those you meet.

Actually, anytime I'm somewhere there's a microphone, I will likely ask if I can borrow it! One time, I was in a restaurant where about 60 military men and women were eating. I asked the manager for the microphone so I could pray over the troops for protection. He agreed, and I prayed, just as I said I would. Then, I gave my salvation message and three scriptures, and we prayed again!

All Things Are Possible

Someone argued, "That only happens to you because you're a preacher." No, it happens because I'm constantly setting soul goals and making plans to succeed in my assignment as a Christian to fulfill the Great Commission. And, I always pray for favor and opportunities like these to open up. And, they do! Why? Because all things are possible when you believe!

CHAPTER 6

WITNESSING TO YOUR FAMILY

O ver the years, many seasoned, successful soul-winners have expressed concern to me regarding the spiritual welfare and eternal well-being of their own loved ones. These soul-winners have been trained in street evangelism and have won hundreds of souls to the Lord. Yet many of their own family members remain unsaved. "How do I get through to them?" is a question I'm often asked.

In this chapter, I'm going to explore this very subject, and we'll begin by looking again at a passage in Jude 20-23 that we read in Chapter 5:

> But you, dear friends, must continue to build your lives on the foundation of your holy faith. And continue to pray as you are directed by the Holy Spirit. Live in such a way that God's love can bless you as you wait for the eternal life that our Lord Jesus Christ in his mercy is going to give you. Show mercy to those whose faith is wavering. Rescue others by snatching them from the flames of judgment. There are still others to whom you need to show mercy, but be careful that you are not contaminated by their sins (NLT-96).

Let's focus on verse 22: "Show mercy to those whose faith is wavering." This includes showing mercy to our family members.

The Challenge of Loving a Loved One

Sometimes walking in love toward a loved one can be quite a challenge. It can be easier to show mercy to someone *outside* your family than to show the same kind of mercy to your family member who isn't walking with the Lord. The reasons are many. Here are just a few:

- "You just don't know what my uncle has done to his family."

- "My father beat my mother when I was a child, and he verbally abused me."

- "My cousin has tarnished the good name and reputation of our entire family."

- "My siblings are hard cases, and although I've prayed for them for years, I don't think they'll ever change."

Without getting into the psychology of why people do the things they do, I'll summarize by saying that people behave destructively and hurt themselves *and others* either because they aren't people of faith to begin with—or because their faith is wavering. The Bible says the devil has blinded the eyes of many so that they can't see where they're going (2 Corinthians 4:4). Some well-meaning believing relative might buy them a Bible for Christmas, but to the person who's spiritually blinded, that Bible doesn't represent truth and life as it should. Instead, it only represents guilt and condemnation. And that Bible will likely end up on a shelf somewhere, collecting dust.

We Must Walk in Love

"What can I do to help my loved one?" someone asks. The answer can be found in the simple command to all believers that we *walk in love.* But, rather than lecture you on the importance of walking in love toward all people everywhere, there are practical ways to walk in love toward an unsaved relative.

We often feel impatient toward a loved one because we either live so closely with that person on a daily basis, or we know that person so well we are very familiar with his or her faults and failures. Sometimes, we really have to walk by faith and not by sight (2 Corinthians 5:7) because that person's spiritual condition stares us in the face daily, and we're often tempted to try to fix the person ourselves instead of giving space for God to work a real, eternal change in their lives by His Spirit.

First Corinthians 13:4-8 gives a wonderful picture of what real love is like:

> Love suffers long and is kind; love does not envy;
> love does not parade itself, is not puffed up; does not
> behave rudely, does not seek its own, is not provoked,
> thinks no evil; does not rejoice in iniquity, but rejoices
> in the truth; bears all things, believes all things, hopes
> all things, endures all things. Love never fails.

Every believer should quote these verses daily, making them personal in our lives. For example, we might say, "God's love suffers long and is kind.... His love is in me. His love toward me is longsuffering and kind. Therefore, *I* am longsuffering and kind to others."

You might say, "Well, I'll tell you what—*So-and-so* may be my relative, but he's not drinking in my house!" Certainly, it's OK to set boundaries in your own home where relatives are concerned. But, the manner in which you do it is important. I once heard another believer say he loved being around other Christians—but he liked even more, being around those who *aren't* so they'll want to become a Christian.

I like that! The love of God should "ooze" and emanate from us in such a way that people want what we have. And what we have is nothing of ourselves—it's nothing short of the supernatural love of God that's been "poured out in our hearts by the Holy Spirit" (Romans 5:5)!

"So, what if I go visit a relative, and he's doing something illegal, like smoking pot?"

Well, Jude 23 says we're not to be contaminated by others' sins. Yet, we're to show mercy. That means we can extract ourselves from situations without being rude, critical, condescending, preachy or "holier-than-thou." We can excuse ourselves and still walk in love by saying something like, "I love you guys. I'll come back tomorrow."

I think some believers feel like they have to take up for Jesus somehow, as if He needs to be defended! But in the process, they end up beating up some poor soul with the Word of God!

"Yes, but they're arguing with me about the Bible," you might protest.

Even if one of your family members tries to fight with you about the Scriptures or to debate with you on some theological topic, you don't have to engage him or her. Jesus Christ, the Living Word, can defend Himself! All we're called to do is to speak forth the truth—and to do it in an attitude of love (Ephesians 4:15).

Love Never Gives Up and Never Fails!

First Corinthians 13:7 says that love "bears all things, believes all things, hopes all things, endures all things." The *New Living Translation* reads, "Love never gives up, never loses faith, is always hopeful, and endures through every circumstance." Love never fails because it never gives up. So, we need to love our unsaved relatives. That's God's way. In other words, we can never go wrong by being loving toward others, including our own family members.

We already read John 3:17: "For God did not send His Son into the world to condemn the world, but that the world through Him might be saved." Since Jesus didn't come to judge, we are certainly out of place to judge another person. No matter what someone looks like, smells like or acts like, we should simply look for opportunities to give him the Word of God, the simple gospel message, and then trust that Word to work in his life.

A Personal Testimony

My Uncle Jimmy, who has since gone to be with the Lord, at one time, was a "classic" heathen! For the more than 15 years I knew him, it seemed every time I saw him, he had a cigarette in one hand and a mug in the other filled with what he called "iced tea." Of course, he always had the smell of alcohol on his breath. And, at every family gathering, he'd show up intoxicated. He'd curse and usually become so upset about something, at some point he'd leave the gathering.

A few years ago, Uncle Jimmy contracted an illness that landed him in the hospital. His sister went to visit him, and took one of my soul-winning pocket cards in her purse. As you know by now, this tract and soul-winning guide doesn't focus on the sinner being on his way to hell. (Most sinners know they're on their way to hell, whether they admit it or not.) This tract focuses on the *good news* that Jesus did something about our fallen condition—and we *don't* have to go to hell when we die!

Jimmy's sister told him, "Jimmy, I just want to read this to you," and she read him the pocket card. Then she said, "No matter what you've done in the past, God is not holding your sin against you (2 Corinthians 5:19). The only sin that will keep you out of heaven is that of not believing in Jesus." She repeated Romans 10:13 and said, "Jimmy, all you have to do to know you'll go to heaven when you die is to confess with your mouth that Jesus is Lord and believe in your heart that God raised Him from the dead. Pray this prayer with me..."

Uncle Jimmy prayed that prayer and was saved! He had heard the gospel many times over the course of about 60 years, but on that day, the harvest was reaped and Uncle Jimmy became a child of God!

Uncle Jimmy made it out of the hospital. He didn't change drastically overnight. His spirit had been reborn, now his soul had to be renewed with the Word of God. Uncle Jimmy yielded to the working of the Word in his life and was cutting back on his smoking and drinking. Then, he succumbed to an illness and went home to be with Jesus. The point is, the family never gave up on him. We never ostracized him or condemned him. We endeavored to draw him to the Lord, not push him away from the only One who could help him and give him eternal life.

Stay in Faith Concerning Your Loved Ones

Let me share with you a prayer that you can pray and use as a confession or affirmation of your faith for your loved ones. Repeat this prayer as often as you need to until your family members accept Christ. :

> Lord, I cast the care of _____ over on You. I will not take the care of this person's salvation anymore. Your Word says in Acts 16:31 my household will be saved. So, it's no longer between me and _____; rather, it's between You and _____. And You are well able to deal with my loved one. I have a promise from You, so I refuse to be anxious about this situation any longer. I commit to You and purpose in my heart that *no matter what I see, I'm going to trust* in You and just thank You that You're working and that _____ shall be saved. Help me to walk in love and show forth Your goodness. I thank You in advance for everything You're doing and will do in _____'s life. In Jesus' Name. Amen.

After we share the Word of God with others, including our own family members, our only job is to pray for them, love them, and do good to them. Where your relatives are concerned, you might even want to really surprise them by doing something out of the ordinary, and *not* buy them a Bible this Christmas!

Is the love of God in you? If you're saved, that love is there whether you feel it or not. And, you are well able to sit next to your relative who's drinking and act as if you're not bothered by his behavior. You can simply focus on the love God had for mankind in that He sent His Son while we were dead in our sins and not even looking for Him. Focus on the fact that God has a wonderful plan for your loved one's life, just as He has a wonderful plan for *your* life.

It's love that will win the world—not telling the sinner how wrong he is, how stinky he smells or that he's headed straight for hell! Instead, let's tell him God loves him, and let's look for every opportunity to share the powerful, life-giving Word of God in a very simple way and, most importantly, in an attitude of love.

Conclusion

While reading this book, I hope you have heard my heart regarding winning souls and reaping the harvest of the world which God calls the precious fruit of the earth (James 5:7). I've shared some definite steps you can use on your own to take your part in the reaping of men's and women's souls. What I have presented is not a formula, although not all formulas are wrong. Systems and formulas that come from the principles of God's Word are useful, highly effective tools that the Lord expects us to use as we co-labor with Him in the work. In fact, they are the tools that He *can* bless! The steps presented here are simple, they have been proven effective and are easy for anyone to follow.

You can use these steps right now, and share them with others as a part of a group training. They work especially well in organized street evangelism and outreaches. The important thing is that you study and apply them regularly and consistently so you can effectively take your place in the harvest, not out of a sense of obligation but, from your heart because you share with God, a passion for the lost.

May your steps of obedience further ignite the fire of God in your spirit as you are "sent to reap" and to affect souls for eternity!

About the Author

Riley Stephenson has shared the love of Jesus with thousands of people over the past decade. As Minister of Evangelism for Eagle Mountain International Church and Kenneth Copeland Ministries, his mission is threefold: *win the lost; mobilize the Body of Christ;* and *bring in the harvest!*

Riley accomplishes this mission through instruction, training and raising teams who are then equipped to go into their world and bring in a harvest of souls into the Kingdom. Discipleship is the key to effective evangelism. Jesus said in Matthew 28, "Go...make disciples...and teach." Through training materials, tracts and personal witnessing tools, Riley will lead you into a journey where your confidence will build, souls will be won and Jesus will turn and say, "Well done thou good and faithful servant."

Riley and his wife, Kim, reside in Fort Worth, Texas, with their two daughters, Kiley and Katie Grace.

For additional resources or to schedule a ministry engagement, please contact:

Riley Stephenson
P.O. Box 327
Newark, TX 76071

www.rileystephenson.com

Additional Books by
Riley Stephenson

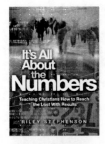

It's All About the Numbers

12 Keys to Successful Evangelism

Passion for Souls

Go to kcm.org
Or call: **1-800-600-7395** (U.S. only)
+1-817-852-6000

When The LORD first spoke to Kenneth and Gloria Copeland about starting the *Believer's Voice of Victory* magazine...

He said: *This is your seed. Give it to everyone who ever responds to your ministry, and don't ever allow anyone to pay for a subscription!*

For nearly 40 years, it has been the joy of Kenneth Copeland Ministries to bring the good news to believers. Readers enjoy teaching from ministers who write from lives of living contact with God, and testimonies from believers experiencing victory through God's Word in their everyday lives.

Today, the *BVOV* magazine is mailed monthly, bringing encouragement and blessing to believers around the world. Many even use it as a ministry tool, passing it on to others who desire to know Jesus and grow in their faith!

Request your FREE subscription to the *Believer's Voice of Victory* magazine today!

Go to **freevictory.com** to subscribe online, or call us at **1-800-600-7395** (U.S. only) or **+1-817-852-6000**.

We're Here for You!®

Your growth in God's WORD and victory in Jesus are at the very center of our hearts. In every way God has equipped us, we will help you deal with the issues facing you, so you can be the **victorious overcomer** He has planned for you to be.

The mission of Kenneth Copeland Ministries is about all of us growing and going together. Our prayer is that you will take full advantage of all The LORD has given us to share with you.

Wherever you are in the world, you can watch the *Believer's Voice of Victory* broadcast on television (check your local listings), the Internet at kcm.org or on our digital Roku channel.

Our website, **kcm.org,** gives you access to every resource we've developed for your victory. And, you can find contact information for our international offices in Africa, Asia, Australia, Canada, Europe, Ukraine and our headquarters in the United States.

Each office is staffed with devoted men and women, ready to serve and pray with you. You can contact the worldwide office nearest you for assistance, and you can call us for prayer at our U.S. number, +1-817-852-6000, 24 hours every day!

We encourage you to connect with us often and let us be part of your everyday walk of faith!

Jesus Is LORD!

Kenneth & Gloria Copeland

Kenneth and Gloria Copeland

CPSIA information can be obtained at www.ICGtesting.com
Printed in the USA
LVOW07s0600011013

354709LV00003B/5/P